"I THANK MY LORD THAT I AM FREE!"

Georgi Vins's voice rose as he held up a Bible. "For five years I was deprived of this book. There is no book I cherish more."

On April 27, 1979, Georgi Vins, a leader of the Soviet Reform Baptists, and four other Russians arrived in New York, freed from their cells in Siberian work camps as part of a dramatic exchange of Russian citizens: five political prisoners for two convicted spies.

Here is Vins's agonizing story . . . his personal account of years of hard labor in sixty below zero weather . . . of mysterious deaths, mock trials, and unwarranted arrests . . . of the suffering endured by three generations of his family as a hostile, atheistic regime tried to break their rocklike faith in the Lord Jesus Christ.

D0816142

GEORGI VINS

PRISONER OF CONSCIENCE

TRANSLATED BY
JANE ELLIS

David C. Cook Publishing Co.
ELGIN, ILLINOIS—WESTON, ONTARIO

GEORGI VINS: PRISONER OF CONSCIENCE
© 1975, 1979 David C. Cook Publishing Co.
First printing, October 1975
Second printing, April 1976
Third printing, June 1979

Published by David C. Cook Publishing Co., Elgin, IL 60120
Cover design by Kurt Dietsch

Printed in the United States of America
LC: 75-18986
ISBN: 0-912692-84-7

CONTENTS

ACKNOWLEDGMENTS

We are grateful to Mr. Patrick Archard for translating the chapter on Pavel Datsko. Other translation was the work of the staff of Keston College: Miss Moira Blacklaws, who translated part of the chapter on Pavel Ivanov-Klyshnikov, Miss Sally Carter, who translated the chapter on Lidia Vins and Lidia Vins' letters to her son, and Miss Jane Ellis, who was responsible for the rest of the translation and research.

Professor George Kline, of Bryn Mawr College, Pennsylvania, gave much appreciated advice on the translation of Georgi Vins' poems and outlined the Appendix on them.

We are especially grateful to Mrs. Katharine Murray, a former colleague on the staff of the Centre for the Study of Religion and Communism, who undertook the final checking of the typescript.

PART ONE
Man against the State

1

A Historic Exchange

Two men walked up the steps of the First Baptist Church, Washington, D.C., on Sunday morning, April 29, 1979. Crowds pressed around them. Here and there television cameras rose above the mass of onlookers. The two men exchanged friendly remarks and smiles and answered the reporters' questions, blurted above the excited murmur around them.

One man had a broad, confident grin, and looked about him with ease and assurance. The other, smiling more hesitantly through his new growth of beard, was looking at his surroundings with the curious, uncertain glances of a stranger. The two men in their fifties, neatly dressed in dark suits, light shirts, and sober ties could have been any two men going to Sunday worship. But only forty-eight hours before, one of these men had been in a Soviet prison in Russia, expecting to serve the remaining five years of his sentence. He was Pastor Georgi Vins, and he was attending his first worship service in five years. The man beside him was his brother in Christ Jimmy Carter, the president of the United States.

Only two days before, Georgi Petrovich Vins, the secretary of the Council of Evangelical Christian and Baptist Churches in the USSR, had been in a labor camp in the bitter cold of Yakutia, an area of eastern Siberia where the temperature often reaches sixty degrees below zero. His activity as a preacher and pastor had led to his arrest in 1974 and to a sentence of five years in this camp to be followed by five years in exile. Every day Georgi Vins had worked outdoors at demanding manual labor, sustained only by a meager diet of monotonous, poorly cooked food, and with little or no medical care for those like Vins whose health had been destroyed by years in prison.

Suddenly Georgi was taken from this vast unpopulated expanse of Siberia to the Moscow airport. Fourteen hours later he and four other Soviet political prisoners had exchanged the bare planks of prison barracks for the elegant comforts of the luxurious United Nations Plaza Hotel in Manhattan, a Russian winter for the warmth of an American spring. Suddenly five men who had been persecuted as dissidents were receiving heroic acclaim.

The first thing Pastor Vins asked for was a Bible; he had not seen one during his five years in the labor camp. An English-language Bible was in his hotel room when he arrived, placed there by the Gideons. Within hours, he had been given a Russian Bible, something many Russian believers never possess. Either they copy a borrowed one by hand or share a common Bible with other members of their church.

It was not many days later when Georgi met the president of the United States in his church and attended the president's Bible class. Carter's free and open relationship with the other members of his church and his knowledge of the Bible astonished Vins. In the Soviet Union it is inconceivable that any Christian could rise to a position of even moderate responsibility. Soviet Christians are second-class citizens; their point of view is not accepted in public discussions, they are often excluded from higher education and promotion at work, and, like everyone else in the USSR, they are subjected to incessant atheistic propaganda.

At the church service that followed the Bible study, Georgi Vins was asked to stand before the congregation and pray, the first time in his life he had prayed in public without fear of being interrupted by police who would arrest him.

After a private meeting with President Carter, reporters asked Vins whether he had known the president was a Christian before he left the Soviet Union. "Yes," Vins replied in Russian. He had seen a photograph of the president with a Bible in his hand in the Soviet publication *Novoe Vremya* (New Time). He had cut out the photograph, and often looked at it when he was in prison.

When I met Pastor Vins during his second day

in the United States, he was clearly tired and still somewhat dazed by the extraordinary events he had just experienced. But I was nonetheless deeply impressed by his calm acceptance of what had happened and by his gentle and relaxed manner. There is more to Georgi Vins than the serenity of the head of a close and loving family or the confidence of an elected leader of his church. He is a man who is at peace with himself and with his God. This peace has been won at the cost of many years of great suffering.

His story is one of harassment, imprisonment, and separation—a persecution endured by three generations of his family: his mother and father, Georgi and his wife, and his five children. But it is also a story of an unshakable, rocklike faith in the Lord Jesus Christ, a faith that has enabled Vins and his family to hold unswervingly to their beliefs despite the trials and tribulations a hostile atheistic regime has sought to devise.

All that began to change on March 28, 1979, when Vins was taken from the labor camp in Tabaga, near the town of Yakutsk, to a transit prison where he spent three days. On March 31 his labor-camp term expired. He assumed that he would spend five years of exile here in Yakutia, which would keep him far away from his family, a usual Soviet policy. Yakutia is over thirty-five hundred miles away from the Vins' home in Kiev, a long, expensive journey, which was extremely difficult for his family to make, even for the twice-yearly visits he was allowed. Now his wife and children would be permitted to stay with him if they wished to endure the merciless

12

climate, but he would still be restricted to the place of his confinement and have to do grueling work despite his weak health.

Instead Vins was taken west. With about fifty others, he rode across Russia in a cattle car so crammed to capacity that there was little light or air to breathe. The journey lasted for three weeks, ending on April 25, when they arrived in Tyumen, a town in western Siberia, about halfway between Kiev and Yakutsk. Although Vins was still nearly fifteen hundred miles from his family, he was pleased to be moving toward home.

But Vins was closer to his family than he suspected. His wife, Nadezhda, had guessed his destination and arrived in Tyumen on the same day. That afternoon they talked through telephone receivers on opposite sides of a glass barrier, trying to plan for the future.

"You will be taken to Beryozovo," Nadezhda told him. The Soviet authorities had informed her of his place of exile, a village about nine hundred and fifty miles north of Tyumen, well beyond the Arctic Circle, near the infamous labor camp, Vorkuta.

Together Nadezhda and Georgi discussed which family members might join him there. Initially his two oldest children, his daughter Natasha and son Peter, would make the difficult adjustment. As Nadezhda left, she gave her husband the usual parcel of food, which he later shared with his cell mates.

On April 26, Georgi Vins was awakened early in the morning and told to change out of the

13

prison uniform into his own clothes. Two KGB officials told him laconically, "Your place of exile has been changed." But they said no more.

That day Vins was flown to Moscow, and taken to Lyublino, a southeastern district of the city, where he spent his last night in Russia, although he did not realize it at the time, in a special reception center for vagrants and tramps, sleeping on bare plank benches.

At 6:30 A.M. on Friday, April 27, Vins was told to get up and put on a suit of striped brown material, an inexpensive East European make, but far smarter than the clothing usually worn by Soviet prisoners or exiles, or even by Soviet citizens in general. He was then escorted to an office where an official who refused to give his name told Georgi Vins that he had been stripped of his Soviet citizenship because of his "hostile and anti-Soviet activity."

Visibly shaken, Vins protested as he had many times before. "I do not regard my activity as hostile or anti-Soviet. I am simply a Christian who preached Jesus Christ."

When the Soviet official refused to listen to his arguments, Georgi reminded the man that he had already served his full term of imprisonment.

That does not matter, the official told Vins. The decision to take away your citizenship was made by the Presidium of the Supreme Soviet of the USSR. It is irreversible.

Then he handed Vins a paper and asked him to write down the names of all the relatives he wished to join him abroad.

For Georgi Vins, a man whose love of Russia

shines through all his writings, this moment was as difficult as any spent in prison. He was going to be forcibly expelled from his native land. Although he knew his family would also be unhappy to leave Russia forever, he wrote down the names of his wife, mother, and children, afraid that if he didn't he would never see them again.

As Vins handed the paper back to him the official said, "At first another country may show great interest in you, but in the end everyone will forget you. Your fate is a sad one. You will always be an exile."

"The God in whom I believe will decide that," Vins replied.

After a little while, Georgi Vins was led outside to a large, black limousine, usually reserved for top Soviet officials, and was driven to Moscow's Lefortovo Prison. Here nine other limousines joined the one Vins was in, making a procession of ten. Although Vins did not know it then, four limousines held a political prisoner like himself, and the limousines in between were crammed with every conceivable kind of KGB agent, policeman, and official. The long motorcade swept through the streets of early-morning Moscow with sirens wailing, then headed northwest to Sheremetevo International Airport.

When the five political prisoners were seated on board the aircraft, two men came aboard and introduced themselves as officials of the U.S. Embassy in Moscow. You are being taken to the United States as the result of an agreement between the U.S. and the Soviet governments, they explained. But neither the Americans nor the Russians mentioned an exchange of prisoners.

When the officials had finished their explanation, the five deportees turned to one another, introducing themselves. The four men who sat with Vins were Alexander Ginzburg, Valentyn Moroz, Edward Kuznetsov, and Mark Dymshits.

Ginzburg was the best known of the five. He had been sentenced for the third time only a year earlier for his activities in the Helsinki Monitoring Group, an unofficial body that compiled reports on Soviet violations of human rights after the signing of the Helsinki Agreements in 1975 and for distributing money from the exiled writer Alexander Solzhenitsyn to help the families of Soviet political and religious prisoners. Ginzburg, a member of the Russian Orthodox Church, had done a great deal to help Georgi Vins's Baptist group and other persecuted Protestant minority groups. Ironically, Vins, who had been cut off from such information for five years, was probably not aware of all Ginzburg had done.

Although the KGB officials guarding them discouraged conversation, Vins was able to talk quietly to Valentyn Moroz, an Orthodox Christian who sat just behind him. Moroz is an intense Ukrainian patriot who has fought for the preservation of the Ukrainian language, culture, and traditions in the midst of the Soviet government's strong "russification" campaign. He was arrested as part of Moscow's repression of dissident Ukrainian intellectuals and had served nine years of a fourteen-year term that had involved many harrowing experiences, including an attempt to commit him to a psychiatric hospital.

The other two passengers, Kuznetsov and Dymshits, were members of a Jewish group dubbed the "Leningrad hijackers," who attempted to hijack a plane in 1970 to Sweden or Finland so they could escape to Israel. The desperate plan was devised after years of applying for the right to emigrate to Israel legally. Jewish emigration has become possible in recent years, although Jews who apply still face many difficulties before they may leave.

These two members of the Leningrad hijackers finally left for Israel the Sunday after they reached New York and were met with a tumultuous welcome from Prime Minister Begin and crowds of Israelis.

The Russian plane carrying the five political prisoners finally landed at the Kennedy International Airport and taxied to an isolated hangar. The five deportees walked down a ramp at one end of the aircraft. At the same time, two Soviet spies, Rudolf Chernyayev and Valdik Enger, walked up a ramp at the other end. They had been convicted of trying to buy classified American military information while employed at the United Nations Secretariat and had been sentenced to fifty years' imprisonment.

This quiet procedure was a unique occasion. This was the first time Soviet citizens had been exchanged for Soviet citizens held by a Western state, and the first time such a large number of Soviet dissenters had been expelled from their country. Georgi Vins is the first person imprisoned specifically for Christian activity to be expelled from the Soviet Union.

The negotiations for the exchange appear to have been conducted under conditions of total secrecy between the White House and the Soviet ambassador to the United States, Anatoli Dobrynin. Why the Soviets decided to release prisoners to the West and why these five were chosen will probably never be known. It may be that the Russians wanted to give President Carter some good publicity to help him persuade Congress to ratify the SALT treaty on the limitation of nuclear arms so the projected Brezhnev-Carter summit meeting could take place. With President Brezhnev likely to retire or even die quite soon because of increasingly poor health, both sides may have been anxious to conclude negotiations before being plunged into the uncharted waters of a new and unknown Soviet leader or leaders. All this can only be speculation.

However, the exchange of prisoners of conscience for spies, with the implication of some kind of equality between them, is not the ideal way for such brave men to be released. Neither is it acceptable that they should have been expelled without their consent and with no prospect of returning. Despite these reservations, the exchange does show that Carter's human rights policy is not just a vote-catcher, but something he truly believes in.

The families of these deported men had no idea of their dramatic flight. Mrs. Nadezhda Vins

18

heard of the exchange as she listened to a foreign radio station that broadcasts into the Soviet Union in Russian and other languages. Millions of Soviet citizens rely on these broadcasts for a complete report of international news, which is free from the heavy censorship of the Soviet press.

Once she had heard the astonishing announcement, Nadezhda Vins went to a local official in Kiev and asked if she and her family would be allowed to join her husband. She was told that they would.

This unusual release ended three generations of persecution for the Vins' family. The story begins with Peter Vins's three prison terms and his eventual death in a Stalinist labor camp, Georgi's earliest childhood memories. It is followed by Georgi's own diary of his first imprisonment between 1966 and 1969 and a brief account by his mother, Lidia, of her term in a labor camp at the age of sixty-five, from 1970 to 1973. These three experiences form the second part of this book, ''A Family Chronicle.''

The third part, ''Faithful Servants of God,'' consists of short biographies of a number of leading Russian Baptists in the twentieth century. Extracts from their letters, sermons, and articles are included. This essay is a mine of information about the lives of believers in the capital of Moscow and in remote villages, in the central offices of the Baptist Union and in small Baptist communities in the Far East and Siberia. It shows how their lives were at the mercy of the fluctuations of state policy, how eagerly they seized the opportunity to preach the gospel in the breathing space just after the Revolution, and how with the beginning of persecution in 1929 many of them were led off to prisons and labor camps and few returned. It is a testimony to the faith and courage of men and women who morning by morning faced the bleak reality of treading the thorny path of Christ through the frozen wastelands of Soviet labor camps. Fragmentary though it is, "Faithful Servants of God" provides many new glimpses into the history of suffering of the Soviet Baptists.

The term *Baptist* in the Soviet Union is commonly, though loosely, used to refer to a member of the Evangelical Christian-Baptist (ECB) Church. This is the official name of the church formed by the amalgamation of the Evangelical Christians with the Baptists under the Soviet regime. The official governing body of the church is the All-Union Council of Evangelical Christians-Baptists (AUCECB).

In 1960 the All-Union Council published a "Letter of Instructions" and the "New Statutes," which in Georgi Vins's opinion threatened to allow the state to suffocate church life. From this time until 1964, Georgi Vins and others protested these documents to the state authorities, the All-Union Council, and believers throughout the Soviet Union. Finally the Reform Baptists broke from the Council on September 18 and 19, 1965, at a secret meeting in Moscow, adopting the name, Council of Churches of Evangelical Christians-Baptists. Soviet atheists called this opposition movement the *Initsiativniki,* but others usually refer to them as "Reform Baptists."

This group persistently asked the government for official recognition and permission to hold a congress. But their requests were not met. Finally they held a public demonstration on May 16 and 17, 1966. Two days later, when many of their number had been imprisoned and no action taken, Vins and the other chief leader, Gennadi Kryuchkov, walked boldly into the offices of the Central Committee of the Communist Party to represent the suppressed demonstrators. They were arrested immediately and held with about thirty other demonstrators in Lefortovo Prison.

On November 29 and 30, 1966, Vins and Kryuchkov were subjected to a long, grueling trial with almost no break for rest or meals, and sentenced to three years imprisonment.

The Reform Baptists continued to have great difficulty registering their churches or prayer houses, as they often call them, with the state authorities. A church in the Soviet Union can not function legally without being registered by the state, so the Reform Baptists were driven to worship illegally in private houses or out in the forests. This frequently led to the breaking up of meetings, arrests, fines, and imprisonment. In the mid-sixties there were usually about three hundred Reform Baptists in prison, a figure that has decreased considerably since 1976-77 to between thirty and forty. Western protests seem to have influenced the Soviet government to ease its religious persecution. A handful of Reform Baptist churches have now been registered, including Georgi Vins's own church in Kiev.

Despite some reports of local acts of reconciliation in recent years, there is still strong feeling on both sides of the Baptist schism. Georgi Vins strongly disagrees with the policies of the All-Union Council, believing that they have betrayed the ideals for which he and his family have suffered so bitterly and so long.*

"Attempts to practice the Baptist belief in the total separation of church and state have had hard treatment in the Soviet Union.

Baptists who follow Soviet rules can hold worship services, but the government forbids them to preach the Word of God in public. Parents encounter great difficulty in even giving their own children religious instruction," Vins says.

Although the Reform Baptists have been driven into resisting Moscow's strictures, Georgi Vins maintains that they are not political dissidents. "In accordance with biblical teaching, we believe that every authority is ultimately from God and that we are obliged to submit ourselves to such authority on all civil matters. To work. To pay taxes. To show respect to the government. But when it is a question of faith, then we submit ourselves to God alone."

The story Georgi Vins tells in this book ends in 1969 when Vins was released from his first prison term. What happened after that is verified by a number of documents that have been sent to Keston College in England by a group within the Reform Baptists called the Council of Prisoners' Relatives.

After his release in 1969, Georgi Vins underwent two operations to regain his health. Soon he again became an active leader in the Council of Churches. At its Congress held in Tula on December 6, 1969, Vins was elected secretary, Gennadi Kryuchkov, chairman. With this office and his election as an officer of the Kiev community, Georgi should have been exempt from any obligation to do secular work. However, on January 21, 1970, he was sentenced to one year of forced labor. He was able to live at home, but was forced to "clock in" at a Kiev factory without the usual wages.

By June or July the Soviet government was preparing a new criminal case against Vins. In August of 1970, he was summoned to a district procuracy in Kiev. He refused to go. Instead he wrote a letter to the procurator saying that persecution against him was continuing despite his position as an officer of the church. Because it was evident that further criminal charges would be brought against him, he was going to leave the factory and go back to full-time ministry.

For the next three years, Georgi Vins traveled throughout the Soviet Union, preaching the gospel and hiding from the KGB who were constantly looking for him. He saw his family only occasionally.

On March 30, 1974, in Novosibirsk, Georgi Vins was taken from a train by men in plain clothes who did not show a warrant for his arrest. He was held on suspicion of theft since he carried two large briefcases until a KGB agent arrived the next day. Then he was flown to Kiev in a special plane and held in prison incommunicado, a usual procedure for prisoners awaiting trial.

During the months that followed, both the Christian-Baptist church and his family made several appeals on his behalf—asking to visit him and expressing their concern about his health. Andrei Sakharov, founder of the unofficial Human Rights Committee in Moscow, made two appeals on Vins's behalf—the first time this committee had ever made a separate statement in defense of a Baptist. These appeals created a link between the Baptists, who were the first to organize regular human rights appeals, and the Human Rights Committee, which has gained worldwide prestige in recent years.

The World Council of Churches, the Baptist World Alliance, United States senators, the International Commission of Jurists, and a number of Christian organizations working on behalf of Christians in the Soviet Union and Eastern Europe echoed Sakharov's appeals with pleas of their own. And when Lidia Vins requested that her son be represented by a Christian lawyer from the West because there was no Christian attorney in the USSR, a Russian-speaking Norwegian lawyer, Alf Haerem, offered to defend Vins at his trial. He was refused a Soviet visa.

The trial finally began on January 27, 1975. Vins had been held in pretrial detention for more than the maximum nine months specified under Soviet law. Many believers were excluded from the courtroom, and Vins's own family had difficulty gaining entrance.

During the five days of the trial, Vins made eighteen petitions to the court, all of which were rejected. A transcript of the proceedings was made by believers who were present, and Lidia Vins has written a personal account of the trial. From these reports, the bill of indictment, and Georgi Vins's appeal, controversial procedures have been documented.

The trial began with Vins objecting to his defense attorney, Luzhenko, who was a non-Christian. Vins felt that Luzhenko was not competent to present his case, because it touched on questions of the Evangelical Christian-Baptist denomination. Luzhenko agreed and withdrew. Vins then refused to conduct his own defense, because the attorney he had requested, Alf Haerem, had been denied a visa. He refused to regard the court as competent and declined to take part in the trial.

Vins said his arrest and pretrial detention were illegal because he had been taken by plainclothesmen without an arrest warrant. He described the "psychological and physical terror" a cell mate had inflicted on him for two of the ten months he had been imprisoned.

One of the eighteen petitions Vins presented was a request that the Christian literature, which had been submitted as evidence and had been examined by a scientific, atheistic committee, receive a second evaluation from a Christian point of view. This, as all the other eighteen petitions, was refused.

Only five of the eighteen witnesses were believers. The majority did not know Georgi Vins personally, and according to the believers present, many of them contradicted evidence they had given at the pretrial investigation.

Georgi Vins was charged under the following articles of the Ukrainian Criminal Code:

Article 138/2: Violation of the laws on the separation of the church from the state and of the school from the church;

Article 187/1: Circulation of deliberately false fabrications which defame the Soviet state and social system;

Article 209/1: Infringement of persons and rights of citizens under the guise of performing religious rituals.

The specific charges and Vins's defense were as follows:

- Vins was referred to as secretary of the "illegal" Council of Evangelical Christian and Baptist Churches.

  Vins quoted official permission for the Council of Churches to hold a congress in 1969 in support of his contention that the Council of Churches was legally constituted.

- Vins was accused of helping to produce *Fraternal Leaflets*, bulletins, and the journal

Herald of Salvation, which allegedly "defamed the Soviet state and social system."

Vins sought to prove that the statements in these publications were true; however, he was not permitted to call the witnesses he requested.

- The statutes of the Council of Churches found in Vins's possession were said to contain appeals to disobey the legislation on religious cults.

In fact the statutes appeal to believers to observe the Constitution, but this leads them into conflict with Soviet laws, which in part contradict the Constitution.

- Vins's essay "Faithfulness" was said to assert that the Soviet state physically annihilated believers.

In fact the state had previously admitted that the people Vins refers to (who died in labor camps in the thirties) died in imprisonment, even though they were innocent.

- Vins was accused of publishing "slander" concerning the murder of Ivan Moiseev, a Baptist killed in 1972 while on military service.

There is overwhelming evidence that Moiseev was murdered, even though the official Soviet version says he drowned. Moiseev's parents wrote a statement supporting Vins after the trial.

- Vins was accused of organizing two open-air, illegal meetings.

He did not deny this. However, the reason for such illegal meetings in the USSR is that the process of registering churches with the state (which is itself a breach of the Constitution) is not always properly observed, and believers are consequently deprived of the opportunity to meet legally for worship.

- One of these meetings was said to be held "under the pretext" of a wedding.

The bride testified that it was a genuine wedding. The sermon Vins delivered at the wedding allegedly contained appeals to break the laws on religion. Although a tape recording of the sermon was available, the court refused to listen to it.

When Vins was given an opportunity to sum up his own defense, he replied, "I refuse to make a speech for the defense, since my lawyer, Alf Haerem, should have conducted my defense at this trial. May my relatives and fellow believers understand me rightly. He in whom I believe will defend me—my God, Jesus Christ!"

The judge urged Vins to say a final word, which is a prerogative of the accused.

Again, Vins refused. "My Lord will say the final word for me, who said of himself, 'I am the Alpha and Omega, the beginning and the end.' "

Lidia Vins described the end of this trial:

Georgi went out carrying flowers [Christians had given him] and saying, "Greetings to all friends." By this time there were more than five hundred believers outside the building and about two hundred who had come by bus and tram. They were all waiting for this moment and holding bouquets of flowers. But he was secretly led out another way.

Then all the believers removed their head gear and began to sing. It was very moving. The group of five hundred sang. Everything was still, no one moved. Then I came out with my grandson, leaning on his arm. He took off his cap, as at a funeral. They opened up to let us through, and we made our way home.

After a brief meeting with some members of his family, Georgi Vins was sent to Siberia. From then on, news of him only came from sporadic letters to his family and through their visits. The letters are remarkable for their quiet but strong Christian hope and joyfulness. References to his ill health occur, but are submerged in his expressions of deep love and longing for his family, and of his total trust and commitment to Jesus Christ. Vins was very much aware of the natural beauty around him, a rare phenomenon among inmates of labor camps. This brief extract from one of his letters is typical:

It is ten o'clock in the morning. The frost is moderate—no more than -40°C. The sun has just appeared above the horizon. It is an enormous, bright, beautiful disk in the frosty sky, against the background of the snow-white wilderness. It's so beautiful! My heart is joyful. It is Christmas Day! My greatest dream is to visit a gathering of God's children, to immerse myself in contemplation and to listen, listen. . . .

"On what do you set your hopes?" one of the officers asked me.

"On God and on the prayers of his people," I replied.

Georgi Vins's family became increasingly concerned about his poor health, especially during 1977. When members of his family were visiting him in February, he suddenly developed a high temperature, his blood pressure went up, he experienced terrific chest pains, and his face swelled. In March he wrote that he continued to suffer heart pains, which made it impossible for him to lie down at night and sleep. He suffered paralysis of his left hand as well as the continued facial swelling.

He was taken to the camp hospital, where he was given three blood transfusions and seventy injections of penicillin to keep him alive.

"Mentally," he wrote to his family, "I had already taken my leave of you. But the Lord provided relief. . . . I feel much better again."

But when his wife and son visited him in May, they found him critically ill. He could barely stand, his head was covered with cracked, chapped skin; he had continual headaches and was suffering from exhaustion. They thought he might be suffering from mercury poisoning.

Georgi Vins recovered from this crisis though his health was far from good at the time of his release. In the period before his expulsion from Russia, he was well fed, and was allowed to grow his hair and beard so that, in contrast to the four other emaciated and shaven deportees, he looked reasonably healthy.

What Georgi Vins's life in the West will be like is hard to say. The speed and suddenness of events have given him no time to make plans. First his family will join him so they can come to a joint decision about their futures. It is too early to say whether they will remain in the United States, the country that brought about their freedom, or go north to Canada, where they have relatives, or even go to Europe, to Germany or England. But it is certain that wherever they travel in years to come, they will meet many brothers and sisters in Christ who for years have prayed for them, wept for them, and worked for their freedom in many different ways. Christians everywhere have been inspired and deepened by the faith, love, and unity this family has consistently shown to each other and to all their brethren scattered throughout the length and breadth of the Soviet Union.

Jane Ellis
Keston College

*The story of the formation of the All-Union Council of Evangelical Christians-Baptists, and the rise of opposition to it within the church, can be found in *Faith on Trial in Russia* by Michael Bourdeaux (England: Hodder & Stoughton, 1971).

PART TWO
A
Family
Chronicle

Introduction

THIS IS AN ORDINARY CHRONICLE of a normal Christian family, one of the many thousands in our country.

Persecution, prison, and exile for their faith have become a way of life for the Christians of Russia.

These pages set forth memories of my father, Peter Yakovlevich Vins, a preacher of the Gospel in the 1930's in Siberia and the Far East, who was physically annihilated in 1943 in one of the labor camps of Magadan.

In the section "My Labor Camp Diary" are set forth in chronological sequence, with commentaries, some poems which I wrote during my imprisonment from 1966-69.

I also quote letters from my mother which I received in the camps of the Perm region, and which the Lord has helped me to preserve until now, despite numerous searches both in the camps and at "liberty."

Some facts about the arrest and trial of my mother in 1970 and 1971 are also cited.

2

Memories of My Father

First Arrest

By faith Moses, when he was grown up, refused
to be called the son of Pharoah's daughter,
choosing rather to share ill-treatment with the
people of God than to enjoy the fleeting
pleasures of sin. He considered abuse suffered
for the Christ greater wealth than the treasures
of Egypt.[1]

Every time I read Hebrews chapter 11, verses 24
to 26, I involuntarily recall that these were my
father's favorite verses. Like many Russian Christians of his time, he had a profound understanding of
the Biblical truth that it is better to suffer with God's
people, to bear the vilification of Christ, than to have

[1]All Bible quotations are taken from the Revised Standard
Version of the English Bible, except where the Russian version is
significantly different from it.

transient sinful enjoyment and earthly treasures.

There are no greater riches than Christ, and you feel this especially keenly when they want to take Him away from you, when they forbid you to share these riches with people . . . But people need Him so much!

Jesus—is there any name more dear to a redeemed soul?

You are near to me, as the shore is to the sea,
You are dear to me, as water is to earth,
You came to make grief sweet
And to light the fire of love in the shadows.

Without You I do not need life,
Without You I merely breathe.
You alone are the joy of my soul,
Be always with me, I beg You!

Thus wrote a Christian poet.

Beside the name of Jesus can be set the names of my mother and father. Beside, but not above. How fortunate those children are who have a loving father and mother beside them!

It is a great blessing if the parents who have given their children life have given them not only a good upbringing, education and a vocation, but also their own Christian life, if, in short, they have pointed them to Christ—a man's best friend!

And if the parents were found worthy to suffer for Christ and, fettered, ever to drink to the dregs the cup of death, then for their son or daughter their feat of faith becomes a sacred example of lofty self-sacrificing Christian love, and calls them to be faithful to the Lord.

The first time my father was arrested was in Moscow in 1930, when I was two years old. At that time he was participating in the work of the Assembly of the Union of Evangelical Christians Baptists, as the representative of the brotherhood of Evangelical Christians Baptists of the Far East.

On his arrival in Moscow my father was summoned to the NKVD,[2] where it was suggested to him that at the Assembly he should support the candidatures of the ministers B. and K., who had been selected by the government bodies as members of the administrative board of the Baptist Union. My father was very surprised by the authorities' suggestion, which was manifest interference in the internal life of the church, and refused to support these candidatures. Within a few days he was arrested. As for B. and K., they were elected just the same to the administrative board of the Baptist Union. Subsequently, B. revealed himself as a traitor when the President of the Baptist Union, Nikolai Vasilievich Odintsov, was arrested. In 1935 B. contributed a good deal to the actual closing of the Baptist Union.[3]

Beginning in the 1930's, pressure on prominent workers in religious societies was intensified, and apostates were advanced to positions of leadership with the aim of corrupting the church from inside. My father spent three months under investigation in Butyrki prison, and was then sentenced to three years in labor camp. At that time in Blagoveshchensk-on-Amur his son, who had just

[2]NKVD—People's Commissariat for Internal Affairs. The name of the Soviet secret police rmm 1934 to 1946.

[3]According to certain information, B. was killed after the war during the Ashkhabad earthquake of 1948. (Author's footnote)

begun to talk, would kneel down with his mother and repeat just four words: "Jesus! Bring Daddy back!"

During those three years father passed under guard through many prisoners' convoys, prisons, and labor camps in the Far East and the Northern Urals. In the Far East he was taken in convoy to a labor camp situated on the shore of Svetlaya Bay.

One day in a town in the Far East a column of prisoners was being marched from a transit prison to a goods station for embarkation. After the column ran weeping women, seeing off their fathers, husbands, sons. A young Orthodox priest was marching in the column beside my father. His wife was hurrying alongside. As she took leave of him, she cried: "Vasya! Don't lose heart! The darker the night, the brighter are the stars!" The priest's heartening reply rang out above the column of prisoners: "The deeper the sorrow, the nearer is God!"

About ten Orthodox priests were serving their sentences in the labor camp at Svetlaya Bay, and they worked as orderlies in the prison hospital. They behaved very warmly and sympathetically to my father, and even got him a job as an orderly in the hospital. In 1932 my father sent me a poem from this camp for my birthday. I have kept it carefully. It is very dear to me, because it contains the sacred testament of a prisoner-father to his four-year-old son. Here are some lines from this poem:

1932

Now you are forced involuntarily
To suffer for the name of the Lord,

38

But I pray that you may willingly
Choose the thorny path of Christ.

When the golden days of childhood
Have passed by, and, as a young man,
You turn your clear eyes
Into the lands of your dreams,

. Then give up all your strength of will,
All the dreams of your heart,
Your unpolluted life and destiny—
Everything to His service!

LABOR CAMP, SVETLAYA BAY

For a Christian there is always a Svetlaya[4] Bay in Christ Jesus. Neither the storms of persecution nor the darkness of unbelief are able to take away his bright hope in Christ.

For some time father was in camps in the Northern Urals. He was taken with a train load of convicts to Usolye (now Solikamsk), and then marched in convoy another 300 kilometers to the north to one of the timber-felling camps of the *taiga.*[5]

In 1967 I also visited these places, also under guard. Like my father, I was taken in convoy to Solikamsk, and then 200 kilometers farther north, not on foot but in open trucks under the guard of soldiers and watchdogs.

As we drove along the old convoy roads I remembered my father. Perhaps he had once walked along these very same roads.

[4]Literal meaning: "bright."

[5]*Taiga*—coniferous forest in the northern regions of the Soviet Union. It is immediately south of the bleak tundra of the Arctic.

39

I wrote these lines in 1967 in one of the Ural labor camps, recalling the chains of my father:

The valleys and hills of the Urals,
The green sea of forests.
Here your path lay,
Here your love died away!

You walked through storms and tempests,
And heard the howl of wild beasts,
But early in spring the birch trees
Were whispering, "Stand firm, my son!"

At Liberty

In the summer of 1933 father was released.

Mother and I traveled to Novosibirsk to meet him. Here he was faced with the journey to Biisk, which at that time was a small town lost among the forests of the Altai.

Father did not receive a passport when he was released, but was directed to a place of residence in Biisk with the status of an exile. We traveled in a passenger train. I can still remember the overcrowded carriage, the shouts, and the swearing. Somehow I was settled in the upper berth, where I could go to sleep, and my parents slept sitting up. At the station in Biisk we were robbed, reducing our belongings, which were meager enough anyway.

We settled down somewhere on the outskirts of the town, taking a room in a private house. It was a beautiful spot. Around us was a pine forest and silence. In the winter father and I would take a sled and wander through the forest. I dearly loved these walks.

There were believers in Biisk, but the prayer house was closed and they used to gather in homes.

My parents were extremely poor. A conviction for religious beliefs and the absence of a passport were great obstacles to arranging employment. Many places refused to enroll father for work. Finally, my father and mother found work, but a long way from home—across the river on the opposite side of town. In the autumn slush and the winter frosts and snowstorms it took them two or three hours, very often on foot, to reach their place of work.

My parents were often ill. I remember that first my father would lie in bed with a high temperature, and my mother would bustle around him and tend him, and then she herself would be ill and father would be the doctor.

One day father received a letter from Blagoveshchensk, from his home community, where he had served as pastor from 1926 to 1930, until the day of his arrest. This kind message with its words of brotherly love encouraged and comforted father in this most difficult period of his wandering. The Lord preserved this letter amid numerous searches in the following decades. Through his faithful children the Lord also sent daily bread in this critical period of our lives.

In January, 1934, father received a passport and permission to leave his place of exile. We moved to Novosibirsk. The meeting place there had not yet been closed. I remember how father used to take me with him to the prayer house, which was situated on the outskirts of the town. It was very exciting for me to walk along the street with my father. It seemed as though everyone was looking at me: See, I have a father, too! I loved to sit beside him at the meeting and sing with him about Jesus, who had heard my prayers and brought my Daddy back.

The same year my grandmother, Mariya Abramovna Zharikova, a true and virtuous Christian, came to Novosibirsk. She stayed there for a short time, and then went off to Blagoveshchensk, taking me with her for a while.

I met my parents again in 1935 in Omsk, where they had moved. At that time the prayer house in the town had already been taken away. The believers had built it on the bank of the River Om. Now mounted militia had been quartered there. The believers began to meet in a small private home on the outskirts of the town, behind the station. In those years there were still no streetcars in Omsk and it was a very long and difficult journey to reach the meeting.

My father used to visit meetings of believers and he continued to witness about Christ. Furthermore, he visited believers at home: he encouraged, comforted, and strengthened those who had weakened spiritually. With him went his friend Anton Pavlovich Martynenko, an evangelist of the Far East Union of Christians Baptists, the father of a large family, who had already suffered exile in the Far East for the Word of God and had found a temporary haven in Omsk. Anton Pavlovich was tall, with an open, courageous face; he was a most wonderful Christian, always joyful, never downhearted, a true servant of the Lord.

They worked during the day, my father in the administrative office of the town pharmacy, and Anton Pavlovich as a carpenter on one of the construction sites. But they devoted every evening to the encouragement and comfort of the believers in that difficult time for the church. In 1935 a prominent worker in the Far East Baptist Union, V. P., arrived in Omsk with his family. He did not join in the believers' meetings, but stayed at home and tried to spread his mood of depression among the others. My father and Anton Pavlovich had to talk a great deal with him, trying to encourage V. P. and lessen his influence of fear and time-serving. However, V. P. never fulfilled his role as a minister . . . .

Father's Sermons

I have preserved rough copies of my father's sermons, and his summaries and letters to believers written in Omsk in 1935. I include one of his sermons (in abridged form), and one of his letters to believers.

The Completion of What Is Lacking in Christ's Afflictions

"Now I rejoice in my sufferings for your sake, and in my flesh I complete what is lacking in Christ's afflictions for the sake of his body, that is, the church" (Col. 1: 24).

At a superficial reading the words of our text lead to a certain perplexity, and the question arises: surely Christ's sacrifice is sufficient for our salvation? Surely Paul's sufferings were not necessary for the fulfillment of what is lacking?

Let us look more closely at these questions. Scripture says clearly that the sacrifice of Christ is entirely sufficient for our salvation: "He himself bore our sins in his body on the tree" (I Peter 2: 24). "It is finished" (John 19: 30). These words uttered by the

Lord on the cross are an undeniable proof of the sufficiency of this suffering for our salvation (Heb. 10: 10-14). Paul says that by his sufferings he supplies "what is lacking in Christ's afflictions" for the church.

There are two ideas here which must be mastered.

The first idea is that there is *insufficient recognition* of the afflictions of Christ: of the afflictions which the Lord underwent as He walked with His firm, courageous, sure step, overcoming the sufferings of Gethsemane and Golgotha, the humiliation, the shame and the loneliness.

This lack (in recognition) Paul completed when he endured what is described in I Corinthians 4: 9-13; II Corinthians 4: 8-18; II Corinthians 6: 3-10.

Therefore Paul did not shun sufferings and hardship, realizing that just as he and other apostles claimed their strength from the matchless conduct of the Lord, foreseeing and enduring suffering, so the believers must and would be encouraged by his chains and his privations (Phil. 1: 14).

The second idea is that Paul did not suffer for his faults, not as a thief or a murderer. He suffered "for . . . the church." He suffered for Christ's Gospel. He bore everything "for the sake of the elect, that they also may obtain the salvation" (II Tim. 1: 8, 12; 2: 8-10).

But is it conceivable that Paul alone compensated for this lack? No! By his words, "Us apostles as last of all" (I Cor. 4: 9; II Cor. 6: 1), Paul joins others also to this service of the completion of what is lacking in Christ's afflictions.

To this number undoubtedly belong Stephen, the first martyr, who was stoned to death; James, the brother of John, who was beheaded by Herod; Peter, who was beaten before the Sanhedrin; John, who was exiled to the island of Patmos; and Timothy, who suffered imprisonment (Heb. 13: 23).

To this number should be added Polycarp, the Bishop of the church of Smyrna, who lived in the second century; Jan Hus, who was burnt at the stake in the 14th century; John Bunyan, who spent 14 years in a damp dungeon; and about fifty million others (according to the calculations of some), who proved their love and devotion to Christ, dying in the Roman amphitheaters at the hands of gladiators and wild beasts of prey, and from torments in the torture chambers, and on the fires of the Inquisition, branded as foes, traitors, and heretics.

To this glorious company of the saints, of whom the whole world was not worthy, our brothers and sisters suffering for Christ today also belong. God has had such chosen people in every generation. He has them in our time also. But is it worth enumerating their names on paper, when their names are inscribed in God's memory and in the memory of His faithful people? For were His servants ever such a spectacle (I Cor. 4: 9) as they are in our time?

How then must we, members of His body, behave to those who are suffering in this way for His Church? First of all, we must pray for them. If Paul, the apostle to the Gentiles, stood in need of the prayer of others for himself, and begged for it, how much more in need are our brothers and sisters on whose shoulders lies this heavy burden of suffering. Pray that they may always feel the blessing promised by God (Mt. 5: 10-12), that they may not lose heart, but that on the contrary they might be an example to

45

us all by their steadfastness and courage. Secondly, we must lighten their sufferings, taking onto ourselves part of the burden of worry about their families, and at times about themselves.

A New Year's Letter
December 12, 1935.

Yet another year has come to its end.

A year which seems to have begun only yesterday.

A year which has brought to many of the Lord's faithful no little grief, suffering, and hardship.

A year when more than one tear was shed.

A year when the Lord like an eagle destroyed through circumstances more than one nest of cherished hopes, dreams, and private plans, but then caught us up and bore us on His wings, to teach us to walk by faith and not by sight, that is, by senses or feelings (Deut. 32: 11-12; II Cor. 5: 7).

We are called to live by faith (Rom. 1: 17; Col. 2: 6). By faith we accepted Jesus as our savior from judgment and the damnation incurred through sin. By faith we claim the wonderful "power of his resurrection" (Phil. 3: 10), the power which every day and every hour by the death of Christ on the cross frees us who "die to sin" (I Peter 2: 24) and who always bear "in the body the death of Jesus" (II Cor. 4: 10), from the dominion and supremacy of sin in our flesh. By faith we strengthen our sometimes trembling hearts with the thought that He who has promised is faithful to deliver us in His own time and hour from the presence and nearness of sin by taking us to Himself.

But surely He who showed such care for our souls, and has gone on showing it until now, will not be indifferent to the fate and the needs of our bodies? Having given His life for the deliverance of our souls, will he grudge the food and clothing necessary for our bodies? The Savior Himself answers this question in the words recorded in the Gospel of Matthew (6: 25-34).

In the past year, as in previous years, we have once again experienced God's marvelous care and faithfulness toward our spirits, souls, and bodies.

There is no doubt that God, who invites you to "cast all your anxieties on him" (I Peter 5: 7), and promises to care for you, will fulfill this in the coming year also. So let us cast all our anxieties on Him, whether they be about work, food, clothing, or safety, for God says: "Even to your old age I am He, and to grey hairs I will carry you. I have made, and I will bear; I will carry and will save" (Isaiah 46: 4).

May the conclusion of the psalmist be ours also: "This is God, our God for ever and ever. He will be our guide for ever" (Ps. 48: 14).

I sincerely greet all who are faithful to the Lord, and wish them a joyful day of remembrance of the birth of our Lord in Bethlehem, and also a happy New Year.

Yours in the Lord,
P. Vins

Second Arrest

In Omsk we lived on the outskirts of the town. My parents took a room in a large frame house belonging to an unbeliever.

One evening there was an unfamiliar knock on the

47

door. The owner asked "Who is it?" The answer came: "Police, open up!" It was NKVD agents. They asked for Father and produced a warrant for his arrest.

The officer in charge of the arrest and the search looked around the modest furnishings of the room: an old wooden bed, a table, a large wooden chest which served as a wardrobe, and a divan, which at night was my bed. Surprise and disillusionment came over the officer's face. Turning to my father, he said: "Peter Yakovlevich, I expected to see the luxurious flat of an American missionary, but here"—the inspector's hand described a semicircle in the air, and the surprise on his face changed to a sneer—"is poverty!"

The search was carried out. They took a Bible, a Gospel, personal letters, photographs. Father had a bag of dried crusts ready and waiting. He put on warm clothing. A last prayer together in the presence of the inspector, then Father was taken away . . . .

We could hear the car which had stood slightly to one side of the house hooting its horn as it moved off. I ran out into the yard behind the shed and wept. Terrible grief pierced my heart. I heard my mother calling me loudly, searching. "Mother, I don't want to live any longer!" My mother, weeping, led me away and soothed me.

After Father's arrest the owner of the house refused to let us stay in the room. We faced the problem of lodging . . . long searches . . . Many believers refused us living quarters—they were afraid. At last a believer, Alexandra Semirech, took us in. She was a simple, sincere sister. She had two teenage sons and a husband who was an unbeliever, an inveterate drunkard and a terrible brawler. They lived not far from the Cossack bazaar along Pushkin Street. They owned one third of the house. Of their two rooms, Alexandra Ivanovna and her family took the larger, and the smaller they gave up to us. The owner of the house was almost always drunk. Sometimes during the night a brawl would start up. Then Mother and I would get out the window and flee to neighbors.

Several more Christians were arrested together with my father. Among them were my father's friend Anton Pavlovich Martynenko, Butkevich, the pastor of an evangelical Christian community, and others. V. P., the former executive of the Far East Union of Christians Baptists, was also arrested.

On Sundays we took a parcel to prison for Father. In those days Omsk prison was a long way out of town. However, in the 1930's the town grew considerably and surrounded the great four-storied bulk of the prison on all sides.

There was a long line in front of the window where parcels were handed in. Everyone was bringing something to a loved one. Anxiously they asked if he was alive, when he would be released, when the trial would be, and many other things. The answers were general and formal. But if they took the parcel, it meant he was alive and still there.

Not many people cried. Their tears had already been wept out and grief had hidden itself in the depths of sunken eyes. Some did cry—the "novices."

The parcels we brought were large, at Father's request, so that he could share them with others. He was held in a cell with Siberian Tatars or Cossacks, I don't remember exactly; they were Muslims, not Russians. We sent him many rusks, boiled potatoes,

onions, and sugar. It was almost a commune—
prisoners had all things in common. Father was the
"trusty" in his cell, and the only Russian there. The
Muslims took to him at once and helped him
willingly form a bond.

Before me are a few yellowed pages from a
notebook. They contain short penciled letters in my
father's hand from Omsk prison. Every line and every word of my father's is dear to me. How grateful I
am to the Lord for preserving them! How much
spiritual strength I derive from my father's sacred
evangelical precepts!

April 11, 1936

My dear ones,

There is still no change in my case.

Klimenko has been on a week's hunger strike for
the second time. He has already been interrogated
once. The procurator has promised to conclude the
investigation by September 15. But I don't think I
believe that.

Tell our dear ones to pray that the Lord will
strengthen the brethren and myself to be His faithful
witnesses. It is doubtful that we shall be released,
although our only crime is faithfulness to the Lord. I
believe that the Lord can do anything. It is better to
be with Him in prison than at liberty without Him.

                                    Yours until death—
                                    Father

October, 1936

Dear L. and beloved G.

From September 26 I was summoned twice a day

to interrogation, and the investigation was concluded on October 5.

The Lord strengthened me and gave me the power and the courage to confess Him. They have promised to pass my case over to the special board of the regional court. There is some hope that the trial will take place in November. According to the interrogator, there are twelve of us: A. P., Klimenko, Peter Ignatievich, Butkevich, the pastor of a community of evangelical Christians, and six others—I don't know who they are: but V. P. has been released because he was not active in the work of the community.

The Lord is our defense.

The medical commission came: I have dilation of the heart muscles and a condition of the appendix. I pray the Lord to strengthen you physically and spiritually.

Don't worry about me.

> May God keep you!
> Peter

November 15, 1936

Greetings my dear L. and G.:

I hope that there will not now be long for us to wait until the trial, and then we will be granted a meeting. The case has now been passed to the special board of the regional court. I hope that the trial will be held at the end of November or the beginning of December. Come to the trial. We will be granted a meeting there. The regional procurator and the special board can permit a meeting before the trial. I miss you very much, my darlings. I worry because I don't know how you are and what the state of your health is, Lidia. In my thoughts I dwell with delight on happy moments spent with you. To my deep regret there were not so very many of them . . .

The last seven months which I have spent in this school of patience have taught me a great deal, I hope for my whole life.

Don't worry about me; I am in good spiritual health and relatively well physically. You can write to me here by post at the prison address: 3 Investigation Block, cell No. 12.

Greetings to Mother and all our dear ones. I kiss you affectionately.

Father
Vins P. Ya.
Cell No. 12

December 15, 1936
My beloved darlings:

Today I have just (at four o'clock in the afternoon) received your precious letter of November 29—this is the first letter. As I was reading it the tears kept welling up in my eyes and it cost an enormous effort of will to hide them from my comrades in the cell. But it was not because I was downhearted, but on account of your love for me, which shines through your letter. Your wish that I should not be downhearted entirely coincides with mine, and so far I have not been. The prison authorities treat me well. The comrades in the cell treat me very well, as in the interests of hygiene we have marked off a corner for smoking, which all the smokers conscientiously observe. In a word, I live tolerably well, for no thefts or excesses are committed in our cell, and if you were with me, and moreover if we were free, then it would be quite all right. However, it is as it is, only don't worry about me. I would like just one thing, to be sentenced soon, for I don't expect to be released. The time of the trial is not yet known, but all the same I hope that it will take place soon.

I am very satisfied with Gosha's (Georgi's) behavior. I rejoice that I have such a fine, obedient son growing up. I would like him to remain like that. I am sure that the time will come when we shall be together once more.

I kiss you affectionately—

Your father
Cell No. 12

During his investigation, Father was summoned to a confrontation with V. P., who in the presence of the interrogator asked Father to confirm that he had carried out no spiritual work in Omsk, and had generally stayed at home. Father confirmed this. V. P. was released, although his passivity did not save him later on: he was arrested again in 1937 and died in imprisonment.

The investigation lasted nine months. The accusation was constructed on the false evidence of two spiritually weakened believers. One of them worked as a caretaker and the other was a housewife. Both were terribly intimidated and confused by the interrogator and signed any fabrications, even the most improbable. The main drift of these fabrications was that father and others had allegedly engaged in anti-Soviet agitation in their sermons. Even at a confrontation with father these cowed believers confirmed

53

the lie thought up by the interrogator. It is true that they did not look him in the eye, as Father subsequently recounted.

On arriving home one day after taking Father a parcel, Mother undid a white sugar-bag which Father had passed to her, and on the reverse side were described in indelible pencil in Father's hand both the confrontations and all that the above mentioned witnesses had said. She told Alexandra Ivanovna Semirech about this.

This energetic sister, faithful to the Lord, visited both the false witnesses, who thought that no one would ever find out about their evidence. They were amazed that their secret had been found out, although they did not know how.

This is what happened. Alexandra Ivanovna took another sister with her. They found the said brother, the caretaker, and told him that they wanted to talk to him about a very important matter. He led them into the garret of a large house. There they said to him: "At the confrontation with Peter Yakovlevich you said this . . . !" They recounted all that he had said and what my father had replied. This brother had never expected such an exposure. He fell to his knees and repented loudly before God. Then he told them how he had been intimidated during the interrogation, threatened with arrest, and so on. He said: "I was very unhappy about my false evidence. I lost peace and rest in my heart. Now that I see that the Lord has finally exposed me, I am ready to go to prison, if only I can take back all I said."

They prayed, and decided that at the trial he would tell only the truth. The other witness, the sister, a housewife, came to a similar decision.

The trial took place at the end of 1936. It was held in the large hall of the regional court in Lenin Street. Relatives of the accused and some believers were present. In the hall stood solid church benches, taken at the time of the confiscation of a prayer house. The believers ran their hands lovingly over the backs of the benches, and said: "We can sit on our own benches one more time!"

The eleven accused men were cheerful and lively. They were accused under article 58[6]. Preaching about Christ was considered as anti-Soviet agitation. However, the witnesses, as one man, retracted their false evidence and openly recounted how they had been threatened and intimidated at the investigation.

Great discomfiture for the court! But it wanted to be objective: after all, the 1936 Constitution of the USSR had only just been published. The trial went on for a few days, and ended with the release of all the accused on the signing of an undertaking not to leave the district. The case was passed to the NKVD for reinvestigation.

At the end of the trial the judge addressed my father: "You are a man with education, but you concern yourself with faith-dope!" interrupting the judge, Father replied: "I beg you not to insult our faith. Faith in God is the purpose of my life!"

Father was free!

Nine months had passed since his arrest, but that day there was joy, with tears and embraces. I was dragged into the hall too (I had not been admitted

[6]Article 58 was included in the division of the Criminal Code dealing with "crimes against the state." Those charged under it were not recognized as political offenders, but treated as criminals. Its fourteen sections were widely applied in the 1930's to cover every aspect of life.

during the trial). Father had grown thin, his clothes smelled unpleasantly of prison, but what did I care about that, it was my Daddy, my very own, my own! He lifted me up in his arms and said: "How big you are! Your legs reach right down to the ground!" Carefully he set me down.

We all went home. Toward evening a small group of believers gathered. Fervent prayers were addressed to our Heavenly Father. Then far into the night Father told us all he had been through.

Last Days of Freedom

After his release Father began trying to find work. But everywhere he was turned down . . . Other brothers were in the same position. Then they formed a carpenters' team of fifteen men (all believers) and the whole team was contracted to a building office for work. Our family's material position improved slightly.

By that time meetings in Omsk had been forbidden. The small prayer house behind the station was closed. But there were about a thousand believers in Omsk. Some of them began to leave. Some, frightened, stayed at home and grew spiritually cold.

Part of the brotherhood, my father among them, continued to visit believers and conducted small meetings. The doors of our house were scarcely ever closed. Every day believers kept coming for advice and for spiritual support. The owner of the house (an unbeliever) greatly respected Father and did not obstruct the visits.

Some people tried to frighten Father and his friend Anton Pavlovich with stories about the new wave of arrests of believers throughout the whole country—and to this Anton Pavlovich replied with a smile: "Here we are guests! Soon we will go home again—to prison!" They used every day of freedom for preaching the Gospel and encouraging believers.

At this time nearly all the churches and prayer houses throughout the country were closed. Thousands of Christians of different denominations were thrown into prisons and labor camps for their faith. I was constantly hearing that this brother had been arrested and that those had been searched. Husbands and sons, fathers and mothers, Bibles and Gospels were taken away.

And so I came into communion with the persecuted Church of Christ in Russia!

I was full of joy to see father at home, but I sensed that it was only for a short while. Soon a new parting was in view. Once again warm clothing was prepared; again rusks were dried.

One evening I observed my parents cutting up a small Gospel into several parts and sewing it in sections into a coat collar, into the lining, and into warm, quilted trousers. I understood it all: the parting was near.

Often father would take me on his knees and the three of us would sing his favorite hymn: "I love Thy house, O Lord!" A Siberian snowstorm raged outside the windows, the wind howled drearily, but in our little room it was warm and cozy. We were happy: Father was with us. I sang together with my father:

I love Thy house, O Lord,
The palace of Thy love.
I love the Church of people
Redeemed by Christ!

Third Arrest

One evening after coming home from work, Father had his supper and went out visiting. Immediately after he had left, a car with NKVD agents drew up outside the house. They came inside and showed my mother a warrant for Father's arrest and for a search. Once more our last spiritual literature and letters were confiscated. The search was short. Meanwhile Mother was preparing food for Father's journey.

Father came home late in the evening. He was very calm. We too were calm. We prayed, Father embraced me and Mother for the last time, and we parted for ever, or rather until our meeting in eternity before the Lord.

That same evening Martynenko and other believers were arrested. It was 1937 . . . .

For a while they accepted parcels from us, and we even saw Father. But how did we see him? Every free day Mother and I went to the prison building. (They had agreed on this earlier, before the arrest.) On three sides the prison was adjoined by quiet streets with little one-storied wooden houses which had the traditional Russian benches at their gates. The first time we walked slowly along the streets around the prison. In one of the prison windows on the fourth floor someone waved his arms. We could not see his face. But it was worth our appearing again opposite that window with the grille, so urgently did he wave. It was Father. From other cells people's faces looked at us indifferently.

We sat down on a bench at the gates of one of the houses and looked at the window. As we approached it Father hailed us, vigorously gesticulating at the window. We sat for several hours and were happy that he could see us . . . But then they began to fix special boxes over the prison windows, which were open only on the upper side. They began fixing them on the lower stories. The window of Father's cell was not open much longer.

One day we came and saw that there remained only a few windows without boxes, among them Father's window. He also knew that this was our last meeting. We looked at him for an especially long time . . . Periodically he waved his hand. We want to preserve in our memories for our whole lives just the wave of his hand and the dim silhouette of his face. Father did not go away from the window for a long time. He kept looking and looking at us. This was our last meeting.

By the next day boxes were hanging on all the windows of the prison. We stood in silence opposite Father's cell, mentally appealing to God, and went sadly home . . . .

Farewell, Father, until our meeting before the Lord!

In the winter of 1937 large parties of prisoners were often driven in convoy past our house. Unshaven, lean faces . . . In dark clothes and with knapsacks on their backs they walked along the roadway toward the station and looked avidly to either side, seeking their relatives and friends. I went out into the street and scrutinized the prisoners' faces: it seemed to me that I was just on the point of seeing my father among them. But he was not among the convoy passing by. With a heavy heart I went home.

Mother repeatedly made inquiries about Father's

fate. For a long time there was no answer at all. Then she was told that Father had been convicted by a closed court (the infamous "troika"[7]) to ten years in labor camp without right of correspondence.

Mother consoled me, saying: "When you grow up and you are eighteen years old, Father will come back!" But alas, more than one decade has passed now, and still he is not here.

He died on December 27, 1943, at the age of 45, in one of the Far East labor camps. Anton Pavlovich Martynenko and many others did not return either. God alone knows where their ashes lie.

Twenty years after Father's death, on December 24, 1963, by my mother's petition, Father's case was reconsidered by the Omsk regional court. In view of the absence of the *corpus delicti,* my father was posthumously rehabilitated.

Again and again I reread father's short letters:

Tell our dear ones to pray that the Lord will strengthen the brethren and myself to be His faithful witnesses.

It is doubtful that we shall be released, although our only crime is faithfulness to the Lord.

It is better to be with Him in prison than at liberty without Him!

In the short days of freedom he loved to sing a

[7] *Troika* was the colloquial term for the Special Boards, three-man boards of the People's Commissariat of Internal Affairs (NKVD) which had the power to sentence "socially dangerous" people without trial. They were abolished in 1953. *Troika* means "group of three."

hymn of the suffering brotherhood which was very widespread in the years before the war:

> For my suffering brothers—for mankind,
> Help me, God, to yield up everything,
> And from the abyss of sinful passions
> Raise me to the eternal truth of Heaven.
>
> For mankind, for mankind,
> Help me, God, to yield up everything,
> So that more swiftly and more bravely
> I may save brothers who perish!

Over the last forty years many thousands of believers have passed through the prisons and camps of our country. Their only "crime" is faithfulness to the Lord.

3

My Labor Camp Diary

(Poems written in prison 1966-1969)

Sometimes the reader
Observes it in poetry:
In truth it is the path of thorns
Of Russian Christians!

(From a poem by the Christian poet V. B.)

May 19, 1966

MOSCOW. LEFORTOVO PRISON—A KGB investigation cell in solitary confinement. Freedom, family, friends, have remained far away. A month ago my younger daughter took her first step . . .

I have also taken my first step—but into prison! The cell door slammed . . .

When shall I see my dear children, my darling wife, and my aging mother again? My world has narrowed to four stone walls and a massive metal door. The prison window is painted white and guarded by a simple grille. At home in the Ukraine it is spring, with an expanse of sky, an expanse of fields, forest, and rivers.

But here is a mute stone grave. My body is in captivity, and there are constant attempts from outside to work on my spirit, to humiliate and break it, and, if it were possible, to buy it.

Through the half-open ventilation window, crisscrossed by the grille, a small piece of rain-swept sky can be seen.

The sky is weeping.

Is it not weeping for us, Christian prisoners, shut up within the walls of an ancient Russian prison?

Somewhere not far away is an open Orthodox church. In our exercise period on Sunday mornings the muffled sound of the bell can be heard. The faith is still alive in Russia!

I walk up and down the cell. Six paces forward, six paces back. The cell is small for its quota of one or two prisoners.

Thoughts about my dear ones and thoughts about Christ—the Savior of the world. Only He gives freedom of spirit and real happiness! Christ gives the strength to withstand atheism!

I am not alone here. My brothers in the faith are in many neighboring cells. Even within these walls almighty God is strengthening our faith and inspiring radiant hope in our hearts!

Christ is unconquerable!

The faith lives and grows stronger!

The Messiah is with us!

Our native Russia needs Him!

On the tablets of my heart I record the first lines

of a poem. There is no pen or pencil or paper. Only the heart's remembrance.

May-June, 1966

THE MESSIAH

Far away from the forests of Russia,
From her plains and rivers,
In Judea was born the Messiah,
The true holy man.

He was simple and accessible to the people,
His gaze breathed sympathy to men,
But in His speeches He mercilessly exposed
Liars and tyrants of freedom.

He experienced suffering and tears,
And was crucified by a wicked mob.
Is it not for this that the birches weep
With their bright sap of early spring?

Is it not for this, as sacred tears,
That the heavens often pour down rain?
Is it not for this that in the songs of Russia
A smoldering melancholy lives?

Do not be sad, dear Nature,
Man, do not be cast down in soul!
On Golgotha is the beginning of the sunrise
Of a new life and happiness forever!

This life was crucified on crosses,
This happiness was burned at the stake,

But, O miracle! Others arose
And bore it with faith in their hearts!

There is a land on earth—Russia,
There are true sons of God there,
Inconspicuous people, and homely,
But full of Christ's strength!

Faith in God like a mighty river
Flows through the broad plains of Russia.
Man's very best Friend, Jesus,
Summons the people to salvation.

Moscow, Lefortovo Prison

August, 1966

The first weeks and months of imprisonment pass slowly by. Despite the very strict isolation of Lefortovo prison, a link between the Christian prisoners is gradually established and functions successfully. I know about almost all the believers who are held here. All are cheerful and steadfast in their trials for the faith. There are now about thirty of us in the prison. Some have already been sentenced. Some have now had meetings with their relatives. My relatives are alive and well: my mother was present at one of the trials. I am told that she was very sad. My darling mother!

Once again prison has visited you and I. Since you were 23 years old your life has been passed in the shadow of prisons and camps: first those of your husband, now those of your son. You have borne many griefs and partings on the thorny path of Russian Christians.

Do not be sad, my darling.

Christ's victory is eternal!

Christ is the Victor over death and hell, and even more over modern unbelief.

August, 1966

TO MY MOTHER

I hear that you have grown sad,
My darling mother;
Once again prison has visited
Our home and hearth.

In the youth of your life there was wandering,
Prisons and exiles with Father . . .
But through all your trials
You did not part with Christ!

Life's task is difficult,
It has many storms and losses.
Once again you carry a parcel,
But now it is for your son.

Do not be disheartened, my darling.
Believe in Christ's victory.
The millenium shines out,
The victory of the Cross is eternal!

MOSCOW, LEFORTOVO PRISON

The investigation draws to its end. The trial will take place soon. There are two of us in this case:

myself and Gennadi Konstantinovich, a faithful servant of the Lord. He is unusually short, a modest and sincere brother with a great, unshakable faith in God's strength and might.

For what are we being tried?

For free faith in Christ?

In fact it is not we who are on trial, but Christ!

We are merely His twentieth-century disciples, and we are saying and doing nothing new.

We continue to witness to the Gospel about the salvation of man and about eternal life in Christ!

Our interrogators, procurators, and judges have not come very far from those who participated in Christ's trial in the first century. They use the same methods: slander, falsehood, and hatred for God's truth.

There is no question of justice.

Atheism, invested with power, creates tyranny.

I prepare for the trial . . .

By now I have pencil and paper.

My first thought: we are appearing here (before the court), not for robbery, not for rioting, not for gold, not for hooliganism.

The trial of Jesus Christ is continuing here today, the trial which was begun in the time of the Roman procurator in Judea—Pontius Pilate.

It is faith in the bright future of humanity that is on trial!

Christ was calm, full of spiritual strength, and confident of the victory of the cause of the Gospel.

His confidence is transmitted even to us.

These first thoughts are lying on the paper in verse. I alter and rewrite it many times, until I arrive at the definitive version.

The hall of the Moscow regional court. On November 30, 1966, in my final address, I recite my poem.

They interrupt me several times. I omit the last couplet.

November, 1966

NOT FOR ROBBERY

Not for robbery, nor for gold,
Do we stand before you.
Today here, as in Pilate's day,
Christ our Savior is being judged.

Holy Prophet from Nazareth,
Why are You being judged today?
Is it because You are the source of light,
Of love, of good and of purity?

Is it because You made a gift of freedom
To sons of sin, to slaves of passions,
And revealed salvation to the peoples
Through the love within Yourself?

Once again abuse resounds,
Again slander and falsehood prevail;
Yet He stands silent, sorrowfully
Looking down on us poor sinners.

He hears the sorry threats,
He sees the trepidation of those people
Whose hands have gathered tears
Of children, wives and mothers.

Forgetful of history's lessons
They burn with desire to punish
Freedom of conscience and of faith
And the right to serve the Lord.

No! You cannot kill the freedom of belief,
Or shut Christ up in jail!
The examples of His triumphs
Will live in hearts He's saved.

A silent guard binds 'round
The friends of Christ with steel ring,
But Christ Himself inspires us
To stand serene before this court.

No rebel call has passed our lips,
No children offered as a sacrifice;
We preached salvation constantly,
Our message one of holy thoughts.

We call upon the Church of Christ
To tread the path of thorns,
We summon to a heavenly goal,
We challenge perfidy and lies.

And so we stand before you,
Or rather, have been forced to come,
So you can learn the ways of God,
That sons of His stay true to Him.

That our faith is not legend,
Not a vestige of years gone by;
It is the radiance of immortality,
For us it is both life and light!

Fresh trials now and persecution
Will serve alone to strengthen faith
And witness God's eternal truth
Before the generations still to come.

Arise, new champions,
For the cause of Christ's truth.
Bear the Word of God boldly
To every corner of the land!

MOSCOW, LEFORTOVO PRISON

Early in the morning of the second day of the trial I sketch out a few lines of verse in my cell.

On the first day of the trial one of the witnesses, a believer from the town of Prokopievsk, answered very well.

The judge asked: Do you know the accused?

The witness: I know them, they are my brothers in the faith.

Judge: Where did you meet them?

Witness: I have never met them before.

Judge: Then why do you say that you know them?

Witness: I know them through the blood of Christ! They are Christians, and that is why they are under arrest.

This testimony deeply moved both myself and my friend.

November 30, 1966

Don't be alarmed! Anxiety begone!
Today I must face

A court of ungodly men
To defend the truth!

To defend those persecuted for the truth,
Those who have found life's meaning in Christ,
My own brothers and sisters
Through the blood poured out on the Cross!

Moscow, Lefortovo Prison

February 16, 1967.

Moscow transit prison. My last meeting with my wife. Where will they send me? I don't know.

February 19, 1967.

Evening. I am transferred to a transit cell. It is full of men, mostly Muscovites sentenced for hooliganism under the 1966 Decree.

Conversation is noisy. Everyone feels ready for the road. We are all preoccupied by one thing: where will we be taken, and will there be an amnesty? The convoy is supposed to be going to the east.

The guard shouts out the names of the prisoners *(zeks)* through a window in the door and issues each man with rations for the journey: bread, sugar, herring. But he does not give everyone the same.

According to the amount of bread they receive, the *zeks* can estimate approximately the duration of their convoy and the district: one loaf of bread lasts two days, which means the convoy is to the Urals; two loaves means Siberia, Tyumen, and beyond. I receive one loaf of bread, thirty grams of sugar, and two herrings.

February 20.

We are sent off on the convoy. It is early morning, and cold. A covered truck—a "black raven"—is waiting for us in the prison yard.

We are driven to the sidings of Kursk station and quickly get out of the "raven." Around us are the guards: soldiers with machine guns and convoy dogs. It is the first time I have seen them so close. The dogs become nervous and strain their leashes.

We are taken to an ordinary luggage van—but inside are sleepers made into cells. On the corridor side is a metal grid of thick wire and a latticed door.

This is a *zek* carriage. We are led into it and assigned to cells.

Our carriage is shunted around the sidings for a long time, and is finally coupled to one of the passenger trains.

We are setting out from Moscow. Farewell to the capital!

There are fifteen or sixteen men in the sleeper-cum-cell. I sleep sitting up, leaning against the wall.

February 22.

We spend the night in Perm.

We get out of the train. Once more we are met by dogs, guards, and a black raven. Toward morning we are brought into Perm prison. There is the usual search, and then at five o'clock in the morning we find ourselves in an overcrowded cell, crammed full of men. They are sleeping everywhere: both on the plank beds and underneath them, and simply in the passageway on the cement floor. We have difficulty in finding a place on the floor.

Reveille is at six o'clock in the morning.

The air is terribly stuffy. Tobacco smoke chokes our lungs.

In the cell is an elderly man who will be released in ten days. I ask him to forward a letter to my family at one of a number of addresses once he is free. I put into an envelope several poems I have written in Lefortovo. Subsequently I will learn that the letter reached my family safely.

February 27.

We rejoin the convoy. We are being taken to Solikamsk in the northern Urals.

February 28.

SOLIKAMSK

From the station we are taken by truck to the transit prison. There is no railway beyond here. But our way lies farther—to the north. We wait for the convoy for a long time. We are held in a small cell, very cramped and stuffy.

March 14.

The convoy, at last, on three trucks.

There are three open trucks with an escort and dogs. Before us are 200-250 kilometers of *taiga* roads.

Somewhere here in 1930 my father was driven on foot in a convoy along the roads of the *taiga*. Perhaps along these very same roads?

We pass through several ancient Russian towns. The last of them is Cherdyn.

Toward evening we are brought into one of the *taiga* labor camps on the bank of the river Kama. But for us this camp is only a transit point. Our way lies still farther.

March 21.

The convoy has lasted a week. We set off early in the morning. In the evening we arrive at a timber-felling camp, Chapechanka.

Here winter is still in full force. There is snow in abundance. All around are the backwoods and the *taiga*. For tens of kilometers there is not even one village . . . This is the North.

Although it is rather late, I write my son a New Year's poem which I composed during the journey. I also finish a poem for my daughter.

March, 1967

Speed forth, reindeer,
From distant villages,
Bear greetings to my dear ones!
A New Year's greeting
With the love of the Lord,
And the light of future happiness.

From distant villages,
Reindeer, fly forth.
Bear a greeting to my loved ones!
Tell them: In the rigors
Of his wanderings for the Word
This prisoner is warmed by love

Through the storms of the North
To the blue sky of heaven
The way is paved with suffering.

My son, never forget
Men who are living examples
Of faith in action.

CHAPECHANKA, PERM REGION

March-April, 1967

TO MY DAUGHTER

My dear daughter, my little friend,
Greetings to you from your Daddy, my darling.
In this distant land I remember
Your tender voice and your songs.

You often sang about the baby sparrows.
The Almighty provides all the food they need . . .
About the tender lilies growing in the meadows—
The Lord illumines them with beauty!

At our meeting I did not hold back my tears
When I saw you, my own children.
I counted those short minutes as happiness,
As the happiest minutes in the world!

My dear daughter! You know that
For truth and good, for bright hope,
Your father is torn from dear and loving hearts
And dressed in prison clothes!

My dear daughter, my little friend,
Greetings to you from your Daddy, my darling.
In this distant land I remember
Your tender voice and your songs.

Grow like a lily among its native valleys,
Flourish and sing, my dear daughter.
I believe that God's Almighty Son
Will keep you with His love!

CHAPECHANKA

A LETTER FROM MY MOTHER

May 17, 1967

My warmest kisses. How is your health? I talk to you constantly and am full of anxieties and worries, but I have not been able to write. I had already received your precious letter before our meeting. It was a consolation for me in my old age. How often we fail to understand older people—their weaknesses and loves. In old age everything returns to your memory and gives you pain. But at all events, man comes to earth to pass through and leave.

The whole trouble lies in the passing through. The honest road is a hard one. I am not talking about financial honesty, but spiritual honesty, the ability to look directly, to keep the soul from becoming distorted, to act at no time for personal gain. Many have traveled this road, but compared to the general mass they are a handful. They are admired more after they have died, but while alive they are thought eccentric, to say the least. The spirit and motto of recent times is this: take all you can from life. Very quickly such souls, like butterflies, scorch their wings in the fire, and for the remaining years of their lives they grovel in futility and deformity.

Your road is hard. I know bitter moments of

loneliness come, when it seems you are on the point of falling beneath the weight of the cross. Do not despair, but rather be assured at such times that the sun is shining behind the storm clouds. You are still young, and you will survive and even forget this suffering if that is what has been foreordained.

But do carry away with you these lessons for life. It is good to cultivate self-control, to acquire the fine quality of self-restraint, even when they undeservedly touch the holiest and noblest parts of your soul. This is the most vital thing in life. I am not talking about servile submissiveness. This robs a man of his dignity as a person and as an heir to eternal life.

I would like to tell you much about my pains and joys but I do not have the opportunity. Meanwhile, all is well. The gardens are past full blossom. The days fly headlong toward the future, and we fly along with them. What will our yield be? As it is written: "For their deeds follow them!" (Rev. 14: 13).

The years pass imperceptibly. You will come home; you will embrace everyone again and again; you will feel the joy of freedom.

The anniversary of your imprisonment is in a day's time. It is a sad and bitter day. Be strong, my child. You acted nobly that day, like your father's son. The Lord will surround you with His light and take away all heaviness from your heart. "Thou who has made me see many sore troubles will revive me again; from the depths of the earth thou wilt increase my honor, and comfort me again" (Ps. 71: 20-21).

May God preserve you! Amid all adversities may He protect your soul from evil and guard your life in complete well being. I pray for this constantly, with tears in my eyes. Let us entrust ourselves to Him, the

Guardian of our souls. Let us set our hope on Him. Our breath and our life are in His hands.

> He knows how the journey wearied us,
> How little we have rested, how we have carried
>   our cross.
> He will take away our burden when He comes,
> The time of bliss approaches—the Lord draws
> near.

Your father and I once sang this song, but now I sing it with you, and there in eternity we shall sing it together, all three. I kiss you and greet all the Father's children. "I have loved you with an everlasting love; therefore I have continued my faithfulness to you" (Jer. 31: 3).

Your mother

I noticed in the camp how the families of prisoners would sometimes break up.

You would see how first one man would receive an official divorce from his wife, and then another's wife would write that she was no longer waiting for him and had a new family.

It was hard to watch the increasing spiritual suffering of these men.

Yes, it is certainly hard to live without the Lord! However, the examples of faith and steadfastness of the wives of the Christian prisoners called forth the wonder and admiration of many other prisoners. Even in their letters the believers' wives not only did not reproach their husbands with family troubles in connection with their arrest, but, on the contrary, they encouraged them and urged them to be faithful to the Lord until death.

And when the wives of our prisoner brothers came to visit them in the distant northern camps, the whole camp and the entire guard used to talk about it, often with admiration.

In Chapechanka camp in the northern Urals I spent three months together with two brothers in the faith, sentenced for confessing their belief in Christ. One of these brothers, Fyodor Vladimirovich Makhovitsky, a pastor of the Leningrad Evangelical Christian Baptist Church, worked until his arrest as a metal-worker in the Kirov factory. The father of seven children, he was sentenced at the end of 1966 to two years in labor camp, and was sent off to the northern Urals.

Immediately, within two weeks of brother Makhovitsky's arrival in the camp, his wife, Klavdia Alexandrovna, arrived from Leningrad for a meeting with him, and brought him a parcel.

This was an unusual sight in the history of this northern camp lost in the midst of the Ural forests. On the whole it was relatives living near the Urals who came to visit the prisoners.

The other brother, a Circassian by nationality, was Konshaubi Bekirovich Dzangetov, the father of six children. He was sentenced in the autumn of 1966 in the town of Cherkassk in the northern Caucasus to three years in labor camps.

A former Muslim, he had come to faith in Christ at the age of nineteen. He had to endure much, and to bear the persecution of his unbelieving relatives. However, his faith in Christ did not weaken, but became even stronger and firmer. Now he was enduring new persecution, but this time it was from atheists.

I will not forget his joy and his fervent prayer of thanks to the Lord when his wife Tonya came to visit him in the North, undeterred by a distance of several thousand kilometers. His happiness knew no bounds. During brother Konshaubi's meeting with his wife, brother Fyodor Vladimirovich and I remained not far from the meeting barracks, and our dear sister in the Lord Tonya waved her hand to us through the window and gave us a friendly smile. She was a true helpmeet to her prisoner husband.

Within three months we were once more on the prisoners' trail.

The reason for this was our Christian life in the camp. In the barracks where we lived, we three prayed openly by our plank beds. We talked just as openly about God with the people around us. The prisoners, and also the soldiers and officers of the guard, showed great interest, and asked us numerous questions: about the reason for our arrest, about our faith, about the Bible, about God. We tried to give thorough Christian answers to all these questions. Some of the prisoners stopped smoking and swearing, and even began to pray. All this greatly troubled not only the local camp authorities, but also Moscow.

The camp commandant once said among a group of officers, and it was reported to us: "Another six months and half the camp will become Baptists!" Of course he was greatly exaggerating, but the atheists' degree of alarm was very high.

At the end of June 1967 a special commission from Moscow arrived in our distant *taiga* camp. In the most categorical way they forbade us to pray and to talk about God. But we could not submit to these demands.

One of the brothers told the colonel who headed the commission: "We cannot cease to pray and to talk about God. This is our life. And if you have torn us away from our families and from our own homes and brought us to the North so that we should stop praying and believing—it won't happen. Even here we shall pray by our bunks and we shall serve our God!"

A few days later, on July 6, brother Makhovitsky and I were sent off on a convoy. Brother Dzhangetov was left behind.

We said farewell to our dear Konshaubi, and it was hard to part.

Indeed, "Behold, how good and pleasant it is when brothers dwell in unity," especially in chains! (Ps. 133: 1).

On the day of our departure Fyodor Makhovitsky's wife paid him a second visit, together with their seven-year-old son. They were allowed a short, two-hour meeting, and then . . . the convoy.

We were transported in a *zek* carriage, fifty kilometers along a narrow-gauge railway. In the neighboring carriage, as a passenger, was sister Klavdia with her son Misha.

The locomotive with its two carriages moved slowly: there were trains carrying timber in front. There were frequent stops. At these sister Klavdia and Misha would come to the window of our carriage and we would talk for a long time, thanks to our kind escort.

This fifty-kilometer journey took a whole day. With the permission of the escort, seven-year-old

Misha supplied us several times with tomatoes or white bread.

After this our way lay along the Kama, the great northern river. We were put into the hold of a motorized barge intended for transporting prisoners, and, accompanied by an escort and police dogs, we set sail. The northern river was beautiful in summer, broad and full. The *taiga* came right up to the water's edge and was reflected in it. It was a quiet, warm, sunny day. From the open hold of the barge I breathed in the fragrance of the *taiga* forest with delight, and gazed with stirring emotion at the expanse of river that had opened up, and at the freedom that was so near, and at the same time so far away . . . We sailed down the river as far as the small northern town of Bondyug, and then we were transferred to an open truck and taken to Solikamsk, where the transit prison was situated.

In the prison we were put in a cell which had just been treated with insect powder. In contrast to the pure air of the river, infused with the resinous aroma of conifers, here there was a terrible stench of DDT powder hanging in the air. One could not breathe. It was like that until evening.

And then, suddenly, I was summoned to a meeting with my wife.

I didn't understand! How did she get there!

It turned out that my wife had gone to meet me in the camp, but while changing trains not far from there she met sister Klavdia, who told her that we were being taken by convoy to Solikamsk. My wife immediately changed direction and arrived in the town even earlier than I, together with sister Klavdia. They set about searching for us.

So now we had a two-hour meeting. How joyful I felt at seeing the dear, beloved face of my faithful wife. We prayed in the presence of the guard. And we talked a great, great deal.

The guard turned out to be a good man. He was an Uzbek. After the meeting, when he was conducting me across the prison yard, he asked:

"Are you in prison because you are believers?"

"Yes," I replied, "for the faith!"

"Why did you take so few parcels?" he asked. "You should have taken all that your wife brought!"

I thanked him for his kind attitude and his sympathy.

The next day we were once more on the convoy. The prisoners were led out of the gates of the transit prison. A truck with guards was waiting for us.

Our wives and Misha were standing not far off. They waved their hands when they saw us, and gave us their blessing on our new and unknown journey.

Dear helpmeets of Christian prisoners!

You are always with us. Our prisons, convoys, and camps have passed through your hearts as well. You have mourned over them many times.

Every step of our convicts' journey was accompanied by your prayers. You did everything in your power to lighten our lot.

Esfir Yakovlevna Zakharova, with a baby in arms and carrying a parcel, traveled from the distant Siberian village of Prokopievsk across the whole country to a camp in the northern Caucasus for a meeting with her husband. Her husband, P. F. Zakharov, was from 1966 to 1969 serving his third prison sentence for confessing his faith in Christ.

One day, having come all this distance, Esfir

Yakovlevna spent several hours in tears begging the camp governors to permit a meeting, which they refused her. But the Lord heard her petitions . . . and she saw her husband.

This faithful wife of a Christian prisoner died not long ago.

Lidia Vasilievna, the wife of brother Kryuchkov, regularly traveled from Moscow to see her husband in a distant Siberian camp in Chitinskaya region. At that time she had eight children.

I do not have the means to describe everything and to list all the wives of our prisoner brothers who supported and strengthened their husbands' spirits.

A hundred years ago the Russian poet Nekrasov described the heroic deeds of the wives of the Decembrists[8], who left their dear ones, their fathers and mothers and, paying no attention to deprivations and difficulties, traveled to their suffering husbands in cold, grim Siberia.

Who will describe the heroism of the wives of Christian prisoners of our brotherhood, who from the time of Voronin and Pavlov (in the 1870's) right up to our times shared partings, sorrows, and wanderings with their husbands for the name of Christ, and gave comfort and encouragement to the heralds of the Gospel?

Who will describe how the wife of Odintsov, Alexandra Stepanovna, made her way in 1938 to her husband in exile in the distant *taiga* village of Makovskoye in Krasnoyarsk territory? Later, after his martyrdom in prison, she waited for long years

[8]The Decembrists were a group of Russian officers who took part in an unsuccesful liberal uprising against Nicholas I in December 1825.

until the Lord should take her also to meet Nikolai Vasilievich who was so dear to her heart. What did she think over and experience in all those years? Only the Lord knows.

In 1933 Varvara Ivanovna Ananina, the wife of a well-known spiritual worker in Siberia, came from Siberia for a meeting with her husband in a camp in Madvezhegorsk in Karelia. Subsequently she also, together with her husband, shared an obscure death in the camps.

Anna Petrovna, the wife of Ivanov-Klyshnikov, served eleven years in the camps, and so did many, many others.

Their heroism in the faith is written in the Book of Life, before the throne of the Almighty. And in His own time the Lord will bear witness about them before everyone.

I have written a poem dedicated to the wives of Christian prisoners. It was thought out while I was still in Lefortovo.

TO PRISONERS' WIVES

"May those who sow in tears reap with shouts of joy!" (Ps. 126: 5).

Prisoners' wives! To Christ be praise and honor
And worship, world without end
For the radiant Gospel news
And for love and mercy to man.

In Christ's eyes is the light of good and truth,
In His words is consolation for the heart,

85

But His hands bear the trace of the torments
  and tortures
Which brought us eternal salvation.

Above Russia, from the Finnish shores
To the oceans of the Far East,
Resounds the summons of God's powerful
  words,
And the burning love of the great prophet.

He alone is capable of giving happiness,
Giving healing from the plague of sin.
He sent us to proclaim immortality,
Although prison and persecution were
  waiting for us.

Prisoners' wives! To Christ be praise and honor
For your courage in severe ordeals!
The Lord be your help in enduring separation
And in preserving the call of Heaven.

The Lord be your help in bringing up your
  little ones
In the love of Christ, in humble forbearance;
In passing on all your strength of feelings and
  faith
And in teaching the treasured commandments.

In prison cells and distant camps
We pray for you and believe in God's Power,
That faith will not be slain, will not be
  imprisoned in chains,
Will not be suborned, will not be subverted
  by falsehood.

Our persecutors, hearing about Christ,
Seeing our life and our faith,
Will thirst for spiritual beauty
And will follow our example.

Above Russia, from the northern seas
To the places warmed by the southern sun,
Is borne the song of the happiness of men
Who have found in Christ their Savior and
  friend!

1966-67

In Solikamsk we were taken to the station in trucks, and then once more into a *zek* carriage.

The journey was not far—to Kizel, and there I and brother Makhovitsky parted.

July 26, 1967

I arrived in a timber-felling camp named Anyusha, where I was held until the day of my release.

A LETTER FROM MY MOTHER

August 11, 1967
My dear child,

You recall how Mary, the mother of Jesus, was told: "(And a sword will pierce through your own soul also), that thoughts out of many hearts may be revealed" (Luke 2: 35).

I spend each day of your imprisonment fearfully together with you. When I take food—God's gift—I sigh for you, because you are deprived of what the

Creator has given in abundant measure from His generous hand to the just and the unjust. I share your bitterness about this new convoy, the anxiety of wondering where they have taken you and why. Where are you now? Whose dirty hand and cruel heart is again wounding your young, but tortured, soul?

At times I am weak and all but fall on the long, thorny path along which it has so far been my lot to journey. But the hand of the Creator of the Universe, which holds worlds in obedience, and the tender touch of His Spirit brings me peace again and again: "He who fashions the hearts of them all, and observes all their deeds" (Ps. 33: 15).

Firmness of spirit is found ever and again in Him—the source of universal life.

My son, raise your head higher: "Our life has not been given for empty dreaming"—you wrote this yourself. When you were born, I wrote in my diary about you: "Yet surely my right is with the Lord, and my recompense with my God" (Isa. 49: 4).

My earthly life has run its course. "We have only a very few days left in which to labor—we shall hide far away from grief and abide with Him in glory." May God bless you and preserve your soul, spirit, and body from blemish until His coming. "Faithful is He who calls us, who will accomplish these things also." I wish that you may have steadfastness and fortitude in all earthly sorrows. "Take courage and may your heart be strengthened, setting all its hope on the Lord." "For you are my mountain of stone and my delight."

I can tell you that we are all alive and well through His grace. The children have had a holiday; Lizochka sings for whole days on end, like a little nightingale. Everything in nature takes its course—spring's tenderness, with its fragrance of flowers, has turned to a sultry heat; autumn has already arrived with her gifts—man alone is restless, seeking storms in his soul. I kiss you with all my strength, my dear child.

Your mother

The first six months in Anyusha were especially grim. During the lengthy daily marches from the camp to our place of work constructing the permanent way for a narrow-gauge railway, I meditated a great deal and conversed in my thoughts with God. In the evenings I transferred my thoughts to paper.

October-November, 1967

MEDITATIONS OF A PRISONER

From your youth you stood up for truth,
Singer of good and eternal salvation.
Now here is the end of your labors—
The desolate *taiga* and the cordoned-off zone.

The crush of convoys and transfers . . .
A cement floor is now the poet's bed.
Instead of air—stench and stuffiness;
The world has shrunk to the walls of a cell.

You affirmed humanism and happiness
And summoned sons of unbelief to the light;
You preached the deathless ideal
And exposed vice and hypocrisy.

89

Well, how is it now? Have dreams dispersed,
The hopes of youth, and rainbow daydreams?
Convoy dogs, not flowers, surround you,
And biting frosts replace poetry.

But through the howling of the snowstorm
The song of faith and love resounds in your
  breast as before,
And a voice says: "Go more boldly
Along the path of faithfulness to the
  great goal!"

Good and truth will conquer evil,
Darkness will disappear before the sun of the
  Resurrection,
Dungeons will collapse, and their steel finery
Will be given to museums as exhibits!

ANYUSHA CORRECTIVE LABOR CAMP

TWO LETTERS FROM MY MOTHER

October 4, 1967
"He knows the way that I take" (Job 23: 10).

I send you my mother's blessing. May God give
you wisdom to bear your cross in meekness and
humility. May He give you strength to endure all
things. May He also send you physical strength. My
visit, together with the joy of actually seeing you, left
a deep imprint on my aging heart. The shores of the
other life which is not of this earth come closer and
closer. Much is being reappraised, much is drawing

90

closer. One thing does not pass, but ever and again powerfully floods the spirit: it is the same thing which from early youth compelled me to decline a brilliant personal career and now, at the time when old age and infirmity are overcoming me, is stirring and restoring me to life. This is the suffering of our multinational people—the sight of these young fallen sinners and criminals fills my soul with even more pity. It seems as though Christ's voice is heard, in the distance as well as nearby, saying: "Give them something to eat." I have seen faces twisted with evil become human on hearing a kind word. What a great task it is to rouse man from the animal state into which he has fallen. I know very well, my dear child, how difficult it is to do this now; this is why my heart is in deep sorrow. I think that He who created man in His own image and likeness suffers even more. And you are reckoned among the wicked. Who can fathom the depths of your mother's suffering? But He knows the way that I take. And your way also. He says: "My thoughts are not your thoughts." Trusting in these words calms one's soul.

Your grandmother Masha dreamed constantly of seeing you at home so that you could bury her, but she did not wait long enough. I am awaiting your return home; I want to believe, as I have done all my life, in the triumph of good. I am waiting as ever for the awakening of human feeling and truth; I see humanity in everyone and do not want to let myself think that falsehood is victorious. May it be done to you according to your faith! Will my eyes see this? I do not know. You must also believe in man. Believe that everyone has a place beneath the surface of evil feelings where the true face of their divine origin can be seen. People feel this to be impractical, and often you look laughable and stupid, but it is a fine thing to remain unembittered by life's sufferings, to carry forth the brilliant ray of youth through life's storms. And "He heals their sorrows"; "Comfort, comfort my people." These are the instructions which I leave you. "Speak tenderly to Jerusalem" (Isa. 40: 2). Let this be your feeling and your language. You are still young and have the whole of your life before you. How I would love to see your bright soul shining in your eyes with hope and faith. Oh, my dear child! May God keep you in His powerful hand. I wish you peace in your soul. Remember Nadson's verse:

My friend, my brother, my weary,
    suffering brother,
Whoever you are, do not lose heart.
Have faith, the time will come when Baal
    will perish
And love shall return to the earth.

               Warm kisses.
               Your mother

October 25, 1967

My dear child,

I had a talk with Nadya after her meeting with you and am in anguish that you have grown so much weaker. Do not hide your state of health from me in the future. We shall go on believing that you will soon be home, but if not, we shall echo the words of the three young men, Shadrach, Meshach and Abednego. As for my own health, do not take it to heart—

the Lord will watch over me. For He leads us not by
authority, but by faith.

Friends! Where are you now? On what
   foreign shore
Has an angry wave washed you up?
With what audacity, what arrogance,
Has it carried you above the fearful,
   seething chasm?

Your life is now clothed in a disgraceful shroud,
Your native shores are covered by a dark mist,
But your heart with its former avidity and fervor
Begs for endearments and welcome.

You must believe that these endearments
Fill the grieving hearts of your relatives
   and friends.
Although you are hidden away, numerous eyes
Watch over you and the boiling waves.

Not you alone, but your fathers and grandfathers
Endured and conquered the terrible storm;
Once the confused Simon Peter was drowning in
   it,
And his friends of little faith were
   suffering troubles.

Do not lose heart, brother, do not be terrified,
Let the terrible storm exert all its ferocity,
The Savior Himself will rebuke it, as He
   did before,
For He is with us, my friend, so be strong
   and do not be dismayed.

If you could become physically stronger, I would be greatly comforted. May the heavens preserve you from any harm whatsoever, so that you can be at home among us again. A heavenly angel counts our tears and collects drop after drop in the cup of suffering. Look after yourself, and may the Lord look after you. May He send you good sense. My warm kisses and blessing.

Your mother

In January, 1968, the state of my health worsened abruptly. Sometimes I thought that perhaps the end had already come.

But I wanted to be in the ranks of the warriors for the faith of Christ until my last breath.

I begged the Lord to strengthen me.

January, 1968

How to die . . . one must also know this . . .
Not as a crushed, pitiful worm,
Not as a slave, not daring to dare—
But as a fighter against unbelief!

So that as I go along the narrow road
I will give myself to Christ with my whole soul,
And never fraternize in the slightest
With injustice, perfidy, and evil.

Hoisting the sail of radiant faith,
I shall race to my longed-for homeland,
And look into the eyes of Christ,
Who has stretched out His hand to life!

94

I shall say with a smile to my dear ones:
"My darlings . . . but tears are not needed!
I shall wait in Heaven for you,
The conquerors of death and hell."

In the vivid light of eternal day
Jesus Himself will embrace me,
And no one, my friends, will ever
Take away from me eternal life!

ANYUSHA CORRECTIVE LABOR CAMP

I have not seen my aging mother for a long time.
How is she? I have heard that she is under threat of
imminent arrest for petitioning for prisoners. If only
I could manage to cheer her up.

I pray for her , . . .

February, 1968

The last month of winter.

But here it is still a long way to spring.

The forest and the camp lie under huge
snowdrifts.

All the roads have been blocked by a snowstorm.

Soon it will be my mother's birthday—March 30.

I write her a poem.

But how can I send it to her?

Recently the link with the outside world has been
somewhat hampered, and I cannot send it through
the camp post. I wait for an opportunity.

Then on March 29 I am told that my mother and
my elder daughter have come on a visit to me.

Is this not a miracle and God's answer to my
prayers and apprehensions?

95

On March 30, her birthday, we are granted a 24-hour meeting. I read her the poem, and how much to the point it is.

TO MY MOTHER

I would like to embrace you,
To look into your kind eyes,
To say a heart-to-heart word
To make the dusk of night disperse.

I would like to set your mother's heart
At rest by my return . . .
For the two of us to weep together over Father,
Who bore torture for the faith.

Rest assured that your son has murdered no one,
Has not robbed them, nor brought them harm.
He has loved Russia like a mother,
And wished her good and happiness.

Outside the window a blizzard has risen,
Snowing up the prison barracks;
Around there is only snow and more snow,
And the limitless expanse of *taiga*.

Winter has blocked all the roads . . .
Freedom appears only in dreams at night . . .
Only faith, as radiant as before,
Becomes stronger in God with the years!

February, 1968
I love you, my earthly homeland, my Russia!

I love your austere natural beauty, the boundless expanse of your fields, the quiet of your forests, the calm majestic flow of deep rivers, the reverie of blue lakes. But most of all I love my people—the soul of Russia. Your grim history, so full of suffering, is close to my heart.

But I rejoice: Christ loves you!

He died for you also, for your people, my Russia. For the span of a thousand years He has sent to your villages and towns His heralds of truth, of good, of salvation and eternal life!

Many have tried to hide from you the life-giving light of Christ's love, or to distort beyond recognition the truth of the Gospel.

They are innumerable: princes and *boyars*[9], Tsars and nobles, formalistic churchmen and modern atheists.

But who can separate you, my own Russia, from the love of Christ? At all times you had sons who in the most improbable conditions witnessed of Christ. You need Christ, my dear homeland, especially to-day . . . .

The Lord will never leave you!

MY LOVE AND MY SONG IS RUSSIA

A bleak land of forests and snow . . .
Garlands of snow tenderly embrace the firs . . .
Between its snow-covered banks the *taiga* river
Dreams of spring and the April floods.

---

[9] *Boyars* were a class of independent landowners in early Russian history.

The white sails of the clouds across the sky
Bear a gift of great snows to the south.
On frosty days I whisper with tears in my eyes:
"My love and my song is Russia!"

The time will come: the rays of spring
Will melt the snow, and the treetops
   in the forest will straighten;
The *taiga* streams will run
To bow in greeting to the great rivers.

The river banks will turn green
And the wind will play above the waves,
The meadowlands will be clothed with children,
Like lush, bright flowers.

A flock of cranes descending to a stream
Will cry out in greeting to its native haunts;
On a spring day, I whisper rapturously:
"My love and my song is Russia!"

Accustomed from childhood to bear misfortune,
I have endured partings, waited for meetings.
Protectively, I bore my dream
Of your happiness, my native land.

Believing in a supreme Love,
Which comes to us across the storm of ages,
Today I repeat again and again
That man's happiness is in Christ alone.

For your happiness I am ready to give up
My whole life and my young strength;
To say with joy as I die:
"My love and my song is Russia!"

The camp is situated among the majestic forests of the western Urals, on the bank of the small *taiga* river Anyusha, which has given its name to the camp. It is a beautiful place in winter and summer.

The beauty of nature is overshadowed by the melancholy sight of the camp, blighted by barbed wire, the barking of the convoy dogs, and the black reefers of the prisoners.

All this is so unnatural amid the enchanting natural beauty of the Urals.

The spring nights are poetic . . .

The spring forest murmurs even with light breaths of wind, and is echoed by the deep spring river, born in the *taiga*. The camp zone is asleep, except for the guards. I went out of the barracks and listened to the voices of spring.

Somewhere far away is my home—the Ukraine, which is so dear to my heart. It is the homeland of my wife and our children, and now it is my homeland too. The last twenty years of my life are linked in the most intimate way with the dear Ukrainian Evangelical Baptist brotherhood.

Good news from my friends in the Ukraine has arrived in the camp. They are praying and waiting for me.

You hear the noise the springtime forest makes,
How the night bird cries in the distance.
Spring has come! O miracle of miracles!
How all around aspires to breathe and to live!

The air is once again suffused with fragrance,
With sweet-scented conifer needles,
   grasses, flowers,

With the springtime song of the rivers
and streams
And the bright fires of distant stars.

How good it is to commune with the Creator!
What strength He pours into the soul!
And the stars whisper: "You are loved by Christ,
He will abide with you always!"

All sleeps in peace. Only the sentry
Stands on the watch-tower guarding the camp.
But I cannot sleep at the midnight hour;
I am thinking of my beloved Ukraine.

The mighty river Dnieper and the bright Desna,
The shining Carpathian mountains,
Bright spring in flowering gardens
And the expanse of the Black Sea.

The kind hearts of beloved friends
Who raised the banner of faith above the world,
Who keep the faith until the end,
Not bowing down to the perishable idol.

God will lead His people through the storm
To the victory of life over the abyss of death!
The spring choir sings to me of this
And the forest whispers: "Do not turn back,
believe!"

April, 1968

In the summer and autumn of 1968, KGB officials
were constant visitors to the camp. I was summoned
to conversations lasting many hours. They sug-

gested, cautiously at first, and then quite blatantly, that I should collaborate with them against the church. There were threats, and also offers of an early release. But at what a price! The fee for an early release was betrayal of God and His works. At the end of September I took no food for ten days, demanding that the KGB should leave me in peace. After my hunger strike I wrote a poem addressed to my persecutors.

December, 1968

TO MY PERSECUTORS

My persecutors, I do not curse you,
And at this hour under the burden of the cross
I pray for you and bless you
With the simple humanity of Christ.

I am pure before you: by word and deeds
I have called you to good and to light.
I have so much wished that your hearts
Would be possessed by the lofty ideal of Love.

But rejecting this kind summons
You answered with rabid enmity.
My persecutors, I do not curse you,
But I am saddened by your fate.

The immortal examples of history
Speak of the futility of persecution—
The fires of love and abundant faith
Burn enthusiastically through the whole land!

My persecutors, I do not curse you,
And at this hour under the burden of the cross
I pray for you and bless you
With the simple humanity of Christ.

ANYUSHA CORRECTIVE LABOR CAMP

TWO LETTERS FROM MY MOTHER

December 8, 1968

I send you best wishes for Christmas and for the coming New Year. The Lord be with you!

In these triumphant days, when the whole world rejoices, how good it is to feel that you are not alone! He who created worlds and the whole universe was incarnate in miniature as a child. How great is His love for us fallen sinners. Never and nowhere does He leave us alone. Invisible, He is with us, and with you also.

As the New Year approaches, I wish above all else that you may have inner strength so that you can overcome all difficulties and not be downhearted. "O afflicted one, storm-tossed and not comforted, behold, I will set your stones in antimony, and lay your foundations with sapphires. I will make your pinnacles of agate, your gates of carbuncles, and all your wall of precious stones." What tender consolation. Incline your head, as John once did, upon Jesus' breast, that He might be close to you. For with Him a weary spirit lacks nothing.

Some are already coming back home, having finished their sentences—rejoicing, spiritually grown up, courageous. Others are taking their places. Such is the path of Christianity. But yet a little while, a very little while, and He who approaches will come; He will not delay. I don't know whether you feel the same, but the days fly quickly for us. The loving Lord has already foreordained when you shall leave prison. His will be done!

Your mother

February 15, 1969
My dear child,

The weather is behaving oddly, not only at home, but everywhere. Winter is very cold and snowy. It is depressing somehow that when spring should be in the air here, all is storms, howling wind and . . .

Liza sent you a letter yesterday. Natasha was in great distress until at last she received your letter which you wrote before our meeting, and it raised her spirits.

How is your health? I pray to God for you day and night. May He strengthen you in health and happiness. May your spirit not be downcast in severe trials. "Who has directed the Spirit of the Lord, or as his counselor has instructed him? Whom did he consult for his enlightenment, and who taught him the path of justice, and taught him knowledge, and showed him the way of understanding? Behold, the nations are like a drop from a bucket, and are accounted as the dust on the scales . . . [He] who brings princes to naught, and makes the rulers of the earth as nothing . . . Lift up your eyes on high and see: who created these? He who brings out their host by number, calling them all by name; by the greatness of his might, and because he is strong in power not one is

103

missing . . . Have you not known? Have you not heard? The Lord is the everlasting God, the Creator of the ends of the earth. He does not faint or grow weary, his understanding is unsearchable. He gives power to the faint, and to him who has no might he increases strength. Even youths shall faint and be weary, and young men shall fall exhausted; but they who wait for the Lord shall renew their strength, they shall mount up with wings like eagles, they shall run and not be weary, they shall walk and not faint" (Isa. 40: 13-15, 23, 26, 28-31).

You also must find strength in the knowledge that "He created all of their hearts and understands all their deeds." We are praying for you and the children are waiting for you. Most of all, as ever, Zhenya. She has grown up a great deal. She is charming, most capricious, and independent. It is easy to get along with her. She chatters on the whole day long and her eyes are full of life and always gay. A stream of happiness flows from her. She will suddenly say: "What, Daddy isn't back yet? Well, he will come in five minutes; all look at the clock." Sometimes in the morning she will tell us she dreamed about you.

The days fly quickly because there is a lot of fuss with the children. I think they must be dragging by slowly for you. Easter is on April 13. May God bless you. Be strong and courageous.

As I write this, everyone else is asleep. I send you my kisses and wish you peace and a swift reunion. Yesterday we sent off a parcel. Our warmest greetings to you.

Again and again I embrace you.

Your mother

I often reflect on our Christian young people. Their spiritual birth is closely linked with the spiritual struggle of our brotherhood for the faith of Christ. Things are very difficult for Christian young people in our country. All the forces of atheism are directed against them. But I am glad for the young generation of Christians. They love Christ with their whole soul and follow Him selflessly.

March, 1969

TO YOUNG CAPTAINS OF THE FAITH

For young captains of the faith,
On their way to Heaven,
I wish for faith without measure
And for courage to strengthen their hearts.

On the way will be winds of persecution,
A deceptive lull, like running aground,
Rocks of doubt underwater,
And the oppressive mist of unbelief.

But for those who are taught by Christ
To subdue the elements by strength of faith,
The sun of victory will shine
Through the gloomiest clouds.

At the sight of the wide sea
Of human tears and sorrows,
Do not desert people languishing in grief
Who have forgotten God!

Captains! Hold the banner higher!
The banner of God's radiant love!
Bring to life on the plains of humanity
The bright flame of the Good News.

For young captains of the faith,
On their way to Heaven,
I wish for faith without measure
And for courage to strengthen their hearts!

ANYUSHA CORRECTIVE LABOR CAMP

The end of my sentence is approaching.

They try to frighten me with a new sentence.
They say that I will not reach home: that they will
arrest me again on the way there, and so on.

Many officials come for conversations.

Before me is freedom.

But freedom for what? For inactivity? Or for
new labor in the vast field of the Gospel?

I am not set free alone. My closest friends in
the faith are also being released.

I write down: freedom is not for idleness.

April, 1969

FREEDOM IS NOT FOR IDLENESS

Freedom is not for idleness,
The virgin soil of spiritual labors is
    waiting for us,
At the springtime thaw there is gaiety
    in the air,
And the cornfields are awaking from sleep.

The morning of Christ's Resurrection
Stirs the breast with a surplus of new strength,
And the message of the Gospel sounds afresh
Of Him who awoke souls to life.

In persecuted churches are triumphal meetings,
Many have tears of joy in their eyes,
And an everlasting confession of God
Burns with flaming love in their hearts.

My friends, I know: for Christ
You have passed in bonds along a grim path,
Even now you are ready dauntlessly
To go for the faith into distant places.

Freedom is not for idleness,
We are called to bear good news.
Service for men has become our aim,
Service for God—our happiness and honor!

ANYUSHA CORRECTIVE LABOR CAMP

May, 1969

RETURN

I stand once more on the family threshold,
I breathe the fragrance of the fields of home.
The hard road is left far behind,
The road of convoys and *taiga* camps.

I embrace my children who have grown so much,
My darling wife and my dear old mother.
And in my hair, grown gray on convoys,
The snows of Russia gleam as a memory.

107

And He who is the nearest and dearest of all,
Who is the cornerstone of our life,
Who increases our strength in the
    battles of the faith,
Watches over us from Heaven with a gentle smile!

UKRAINE

4

My Mother's Imprisonment

"She has done what she could"(Mark 14: 8).

ON DECEMBER 1, 1970, MY MOTHER was arrested in
Kiev. It happened in the evening. She was in the
house with my youngest children.

After she had dressed and got ready, my eldest
daughter came home. Their grandmother was very
calm and cheerful.

She prayed with her grandchildren and left the
house accompanied by policemen.

The first snow had fallen, forming a soft carpet
over the earth, earth so rich in tears and sorrow.

The tall pine forest mother loved so much, which
came right up to the town, looked down pensively
upon the bustling people in military uniform, helping
the old woman into the "black raven." Her beloved
forests bade her farewell . . .

The children ran out into the streets without their
coats and cried quietly.

An ambulance stood next to the police car. It escorted the detainee to the prison.

My darling mother!

Thirty-three years ago you saw your husband—my father—off on his last prisoner's journey, and now my children have seen you off.

It is hard for me to realize that you are in prison.

You are old and sick, living under such a burden of suffering.

My own dear! Oh, if only I were allowed to change places with you.

What crime have you ever committed?

In your old age you stood up in defense of those persecuted for their faith.

"Rescue those who are being taken away to death; hold back those who are stumbling to the slaughter" (Prov. 24: 11). This is the call of God's Word.

Confronted by injustice and human suffering, every honest individual is obliged to speak out.

This right belongs especially to the mother, the Christian mother.

And you fulfilled your maternal Christian duties to the utmost of your strength.

Your persecutors could not forgive you for this! They made many efforts to bring you to silence.

They became convinced that your mother's heart was anxious not only for the fate of your son, who was victimized by atheism. Your heart was wider, for the grief of orphans and widowed Christians was your own grief, the tears of those persecuted for the faith were your tears. It was then that the persecutors decided to throw you also into prison.

They naively assumed that by taking you and imprisoning you in darkness, every voice defending persecuted Christians would fall silent.

But the voice speaks on.

Through a thousand mouths . . .

It is heard at the child's cot where little children pray for their father, languishing behind bars for God's truth.

This voice is heard in the continual prayers of God's people. It is heard also in every signature written in defense of the persecuted, and in each courageous testimony to God's truth before persecutors.

This voice will not be stifled.

It is hard for me, as a son, to realize that you are in prison, and to bear separation from you.

I am even deprived of correspondence with you.

I am deprived of the opportunity of cheering you up and receiving your maternal blessing, if only in letters.

Only a few years ago, when my way led through the northern camps, how much comfort and good cheer your letters full of motherly love brought me! For me, each one was a holiday, full of light!

I preserved your letters carefully and read them through time and time again, sitting on my plank-bed. My heart was flooded with renewed spiritual power and hope in the Lord!

My mother was placed in Lukyanovsky prison in Kiev. The fabrication of a criminal case began.

How all of this brings to mind the years 1930 to 1937, when a criminal case was made out three times against my father, a Christian, costing him his life. It is true that they rehabilitated him posthumously. The atheist authorities were forced to admit his complete innocence. Now, however, his 64-year-old widow had been subjected to incarceration in prison on the same religious grounds.

The conditions of my mother's confinement in prison were appalling. At the trial she said: "Whatever your sentence may be, it will amount to a death sentence because the conditions in which I find myself in my cell are unbearable!"

My mother's trial took place in Kiev on February 8 and 9, 1971.

My wife, eldest daughter, and son, and not more than fifteen Christians were present in the court, although about a hundred Christians wanted to be at the trial.

The court was small.

My mother spoke quietly, calmly, confidently.

The prosecutor raised his voice frequently and showed irritation.

Out of the many written petitions signed by my mother and other prisoners' relatives from 1966 to 1970, the investigations selected four facts about persecution for the faith which the court tried to represent as lies and slander. What is more, they did not summon to court as witnesses those who had suffered, but those who directly or indirectly had been guilty of persecution for the faith—workers in the militia and camp administration who, said what the persecutors wanted them to say.

My mother declared in her defense speech: "How can investigators and militiamen, those very people about whom we are complaining, act as witnesses? Not a single person who has suffered was called as a witness. In this light the trial begins to look somewhat absurd!"

It is not surprising, therefore, that my mother was sentenced to three years' deprivation of freedom.

Taking account of her arrest and her weak state of health, this was almost a death sentence. But what do they care about that, the atheist judges of the seventies? They are repeating what their predecessors did in the famous year of 1937, through whose hands my father passed to his death.

My Mother's Defense Speech (Extracts)[10]
February 9, 1971
KIEV REGIONAL COURT

First of all, I would like to say that I did not demand any sort of international tribunal, although the Procurator called this raving nonsense, but in actual fact I asked at the beginning of the trial that a Christian lawyer, a representative of international Christian society, might be present, and that he might carry out my defense as a Christian. This was my right.

I consider that the trial has certainly violated judicial procedure, as it is apparently called in legal terminology. How can investigators and militiamen, the very people about whom we are complaining, act as witnesses? Not a single person who had suffered was called as a witness. In this light the trial begins to look somewhat absurd . . .

As Evangelical Christians Baptists, our creed is such that we respect the authorities. In the Soviet Union our denomination is permitted because it contains no fanaticism. We always carry out our duties

---

[10]Omitted passages of Lidia Vins' defense speech are found in another copy of the speech in the files of the Centre for the Study of Religion and Communism. They concern other Baptist believers.

113

as citizens better than others, and one can say only good about my fellow believers sitting in this room. For we know that all authority comes from God, but we do not want to disobey Christ's commands: "Go into all the world and preach the gospel"; "Give to Caesar what belongs to Caesar, but to God what belongs to God": "Suffer the little children to come unto me."

The Church is separated from the State. The Church must have one head—Christ. As we understand it, He who came down to earth and will come a second time . . .

(The judge, interrupting: "Do not digress; keep to the point of the charge.")

We petitioned at first for the release of our relatives, but did not touch upon the country's laws; this was the job of the All-Union Council and the Council of Churches. But then we began to investigate what our relatives were being tried for, which led to our investigating the laws. We ascertained that in the first Constitution of the Soviet Union both anti-religious and relident gious propaganda were allowed. Later, religious propaganda was forbidden. Only the words, "Everyone has the right to profess his own religion" were left, and antireligious propaganda was allowed! But even though only "profess" is left, we still have the right to preach. For the word "profess" means telling others about our faith, and not only performing rites.

At first, from June, 1966, onward, we went in delegations to the General Procurator Rudenko in Moscow, to the Supreme Soviet, to the Central Party Committee and asked them to receive us. We sent telegrams so that they would receive us and hear us out. But they answered—do not come and do not ask anything, it will not help you at all, nobody will listen to you.

(The judge: "But they were sentenced, therefore they were guilty.")

Why did we start to write? Someone was arrested here, then there, and then in many places, and so we began to write our reports. We called our reports "emergency reports." Our council is mainly composed of women: mothers and wives, from all the republics. We could not sit around with our arms folded when our children and our husbands were suffering.

Only four of the facts of which we have written are being investigated here, but we have written about many more. Something of our reports should have been read here. We have written about many deprived of freedom and their families. In the lists is a column of "dependents." Basically, these are large families, with 7, 8, 9, 10, or 11 deprived children, left without a breadwinner.

We wrote that Golev, an old man, was arrested. He is 73 years old. He was sentenced to three years but in all he has already suffered for 19 years for the sake of God's Word. He organized a mutual aid fund for deprived children and for this he was sentenced. How could we not write "condemned to physical destruction" when the breadwinner was arrested and a family of many children abandoned? No one (among the authorities) gave them a thought or troubled about them, and that means they were left to die of starvation.

We wrote that because we opened our apartments for prayer meetings the owners of the buildings were beaten and tried. For example, in Kiev, Shelestun was beaten, and we wrote about it. He had a certificate for remission from beatings from a legal commission. Punishment was inflicted on the head of militia who beat him.

We wrote in our reports about the breaking up of prayer meetings with Christians being beaten. Recently Christians have been seized on the way to a meeting, on railway platforms, at bus stops; they seized mothers, leaving their little children on the platforms.

We wrote about the Sloboda family from Belorussia. This family came to believe on their own, through radio broadcasts and through reading the Gospel. They stopped drinking and swearing and began to live a decent life. Simply because the mother told her relatives about God, her two children were taken away from her and put in a boarding school, and she was deprived of her freedom for four years. Then they also tore the remaining three small children from their father because he gave them a religious upbringing.

All the facts contained in the reports we gave in our letters were based on documents witnessed by the signatures of victims or of entire local congregations.

We sent our last letter on October 1, 1970, and I also signed it. In it we wrote of Iskovsky, an old man from the Moscow region, who was dying in prison. He had cancer. He did in fact die. An order was issued for his release so that he could die at home, but somebody interfered and so he was not released. He died in prison approximately two weeks before my arrest.

116

We also wrote about those tortured in camps: Khmara from Barnaul, Lanbin from Novosibirsk, Afonin from the Moscow region (he had a weak heart and eight children. We asked for his release, but he died in camp) and Kucherenko who died while being interrogated in Nikolaev.

(The judge: "The accused must keep to the point of the charge. Why are you telling us all this?")

But this is the point of my charge. I am charged with writing letters to the government. I want to tell you what I wrote about in them. I wrote about searches, about the confiscation of religious literature, when the Bible, the Gospel and song books were taken away. Orders for the destruction of this literature have been passed in court.

At the beginning of this movement, in 1962, 524 people were arrested, 400 sentenced to 15 days' imprisonment for taking part in meetings for worship, which makes 6,000 days in all. Fines of 94,500 rubles in new money were paid for taking part in prayer meetings. Children underwent interrogation.

We wrote our first letter to U Thant at the United Nations in 1967. This was provoked by the fact that our government was taking no measures at all to improve the position of believers. We wrote because we hoped all the same for justice; we believed that at length our government would show humaneness. But the Procurator has said here that repression will continue.

At this trial I have heard from the Procurator for the first time that the Soviet Union has not signed the Universal Declaration of Human Rights. I shall conclude now. I have nothing against the witnesses. They are in a delicate situation. Who will say that he

117

has beaten somebody? No one, of course. That is all that I wanted to say.

My Mother's Last Words at The Trial

My last words will be very brief. I have twice had the opportunity of saying here what I wanted to say. Now I want to ask only one thing: there is a resolution in this case to summon to court all those who signed the letters. I ask that this should not be done. I take everything upon myself.

It was I who took the chief part in this.

Again, I ask the court to take my age and my poor health into account. Whatever your sentence is, it will amount to a death sentence, because the conditions in which I find myself in my cell are unbearable. That is all I wanted to say.

After the sentence had been pronounced—three years' labor camp, ordinary regime—my wife threw my mother a bouquet of violets. The Christians, mainly young people, began to throw her red carnations.

The prisoner's escort was frightened and began to take the flowers away from her, but she still managed to carry some of them to her cell.

When they brought my mother out of the building into the street, where a police car was standing, a large crowd of Christians sang the hymn:

For the faith of the Gospel,
For Christ we shall stand up,
Following His example,
Ever onward, onward after Him.

118

The battle rages, the flame is hot,
And places shake and sway,
Raise higher the banner
Of Christ the Victor!

After the trial my mother was sent off to a
women's camp in Kharkov. Her state of health was
grave. She was led off to work supported on people's
arms . . . .

1971

A LETTER TO MY MOTHER

Are you still alive, my old mother?
Behind the high stone wall
The gloomy sentry tramples down
Your gray-haired life, like a toy.

There in prison, as in a den of depravity,
Amid falsehood and human baseness,
You are overcome by deep sorrow
For people enslaved by darkness.

Often you whisper to God in your prayers,
Wilting beside your plank-bed at dead of night:
"Lord! Open to these hearts the way
To everlasting, holy life!"

I know that in your gray-haired years
It is hard to endure prison.
I would give up my life and all my freedom
To replace you, my darling!

PART THREE
Faithful Servants of God

Foreword

"Moreover it is required of stewards that they be found trustworthy" (I Cor. 4: 2).

The pages before you tell of the life of our brothers and sisters, who were faithful to the Lord unto death.

The author of these biographical essays, Georgi Vins, the Secretary of the Council of Evangelical Christian-Baptist Churches, was arrested once more in March 1974.

Another servant of the Church has joined the several hundred Christians who are in prison in our country: a father of five children, a son who has had no chance of meeting his Christian mother who returned from prison in December 1973.

Only God knows when we shall see our brother and if we shall meet here on earth. But the poems which he wrote in the difficult moments of his first imprisonment are full of radiant hope for us:

Hoisting the sail of radiant faith,
I shall race to my longed-for homeland,
And look into the eyes of Christ,
Who has stretched out His hand to life!

I shall say with a smile to my dear ones:
"My darlings . . . but tears . . . are not needed!
I shall wait in Heaven for you,
The conquerors of death and hell!"

Introduction

MAN NEEDS CHRIST. The fishermen of Galilee and the Scythian nomads, the slaves and the free men, the wise and the ignorant of the first century, when the fame of mighty Rome thundered throughout the world, all needed Him. We also need Christ in the twentieth century, the century of atomic energy and space exploration. For only Christ grants real meaning to our present life (John 10: 10; 14: 6) and an unshakable foundation for our future eternal life, the beginning of which is here on earth through faith in the Son of God (John 3: 36). A boundless and mighty development of all man's spiritual powers is found only in Christ. Christ is the greatest gift from Heaven, its supreme blessing. Preachers of the Gospel bear the news of Christ throughout the world to all peoples.

For over a hundred years Christians of the Evangelical-Baptist faith in our country have preached of Christ amid persecution to their own people. Suffering abuse and slander, enduring persecution for their faith, they do not grumble and complain of their fate. They give thanks to God for this special love for the Russian people, which gives them immense power to testify of Christ not only in prayer houses, but also in courtrooms, prison cells, and distant camps.

Believers of the Evangelical Christian-Baptist Church desire to remain faithful to Christ and in no way to yield to unbelief (II Peter 1: 10; Rev. 21: 7).

Not so long ago many people in our country supposed that there were almost no believers in the Soviet Union. By the 1960's the voice of the Church had become very faint. Witness to Christ was bounded more and more by the walls of prayer houses, but inside these houses, the number of which has catastrophically decreased[1], ministers who had been false to God under the pressure of atheism led the task of curtailing the whole work of the Gospel.

But here the Lord showed His mercy. It is "time for the Lord to act," as the psalmist said, "for thy law has been broken" (Ps. 119: 126).

The Action Group of the Evangelical Christians Baptists, formed in 1961, appealed to all believers of the Evangelical Christian-Baptist Church with a call to revival: to purity, holiness and faithfulness in serving the Lord.

Atheism threw the entire state machine against the revived fellowship: the press, radio, television, police organs, procurators' offices, law courts,

[1]In the Ukraine alone, of the 2,000 Evangelical Christian-Baptist communities in 1946, the authorities had closed 800 prayer houses by 1960.

prisons, labor camps, and the Committee for State Security—the KGB.

However, the Lord gave His Church the strength to defend the work of evangelism. Then the whole country began to talk about the might of Christ and the power of His ideas.

Atheists try to distort the essence of Christ's teachings and slander His followers against their will, but the very fact of open, bitter war with God establishes a healthy concept in the consciousness of the Russian people: the matter concerns a living God, for one does not wage war with the dead!

Russia's best people saw the happiness of their own nation only through God. Among these people was Nikolai Odintsov, a martyr for the faith of the Gospel. As long ago as 1927 he wrote in the journal, *The Baptist*, No. 1: "I anticipate a great spiritual awakening of my own people, a broad and deep reformation movement in our vast land that is so rich in opportunities."

Thousands of Russia's Christians dying in prisons and camps prayed for this awakening. God's dear servant Ivan Stepanovich Prokhanov prayed for this in his years of exile in a strange land.

The Christian prisoners of the 1970's and all our long-suffering Christian-Baptist brotherhood pray for the spiritual awakening of the Russian people and all the peoples of our multinational land.

The following pages contain several short essays on faithful men and women who served God: Nikolai Odintsov, Pavel Ivanov-Klyshnikov, Pavel Datsko, Georgi Shipkov, Alexander Shalashov, Pavel Zakharov and others. They also contain several of their letters, sermons and articles.

I also direct my dear readers' attention to the fundamental principles of the Evangelical Christians Baptists. They lay out the basis of the formation of our brotherhood from the very first days of its origin in 1867.

Fundamental Principles
of the Evangelical Christians Baptists[2].

1. The Holy Scripture (the Bible) is the only rule and guidance in all matters and questions of faith and life.

It follows from this that the preaching of the Gospel or witnessing to Christ is the chief task and the fundamental mission of the Church.

2. Absolute freedom of conscience.

3. The Church of God consists, exclusively, of regenerate people. (Spiritual regeneration of members.)

4. Baptism of believers.

5. The independence of each separate local church.

6. The priesthood of all believers.

7. The separation of Church from the State.

Thousands of servants of God in our country worked for these principles, for the purity of evangelical teaching. Many of them yielded up their lives in prisons and camps, but they did not betray the teaching of Jesus Christ!

My great desire is to summon my friends in the faith to preserve and increase the precious spiritual heritage of the evangelical Baptist brotherhood, to

[2] I quote a short list according to the brochure "Our Baptist Principles," written and published by Peter Vins in 1923 in the Far East.

propagate the principles of our doctrine, to know and love the history of our brotherhood.

The letters, sermons, notes and photographs of the dear and faithful servants who were before us; memories of them, and most of all the spirit of their pure and selfless service—this is our heritage, our spiritual wealth, about which every Christian should know.

May this work serve for the strengthening of the faith and the increase of the number of faithful servants of God in the harvest field of the Gospel.

5

Georgi Shipkov

1865 - ??

GEORGI IVANOVICH WAS CALLED to be the exegete of
our brotherhood. His spiritual articles were printed
in many Evangelical Christian-Baptist journals. They
were written in beautiful literary language and with
deep reverence for the person of the Savior. Even today for the Russian brotherhood they are a model of
profound Russian thought in the study of the Book
of books.

In the journal *The Baptist,* No. 1, 1927, was printed
Georgi Shipkov's biography, written by Pavel
Ivanov-Klyshnikov. I quote it here with a small ab-
breviation:

Georgi Ivanovich Shipkov was born on October
25 (Old Style[3]), 1865, near Samara. His father

---

[3]Russia used the old Julian calendar, which was 11 days
behind the Western calendar, until 1917.

was a peasant, a member of the Molokan sect. Georgi received a very strict religious education in his family. In 1878 the Shipkovs moved to Blagoveshchensk. Georgi, by then a young man, showed an intense love for reading and the study of languages. Having passed the examination for several classes of high school as an external student, he entered a postal-telegraph office as a clerk and continued studying languages and reading, being chiefly interested in history and philosophy. In 1889 Georgi Shipkov turned to the Lord. From that time he began to be interested in literature on theological questions and read all the books in this field which could be obtained in Blagoveshchensk, in English, French, and German, as well as Russian. In order to obtain a systematic theological education, in 1894 Shipkov entered the theological faculty of the American University in Peking, where he received the degree of doctor of theology in 1898, and immediately returned to Blagoveshchensk. Here he went to work at the telegraph office once more, and served there until 1921. As well as this he was for eight years a lecturer in English in a technical high school and a polytechnic. This work earned brother Georgi the means to live, and at the same time he undertook spiritual ministry—for about thirteen years he was deputy pastor of the Blagoveshchensk Baptist community, for seven years he was a teacher there, for six years he was Chairman of the Far East Branch of the All-Russian Baptist Union, and for six years

130

Comrade Chairman of this Branch, subsequently renamed the Far East Baptist Union.

Shipkov lived almost all of his life in Blagoveshchensk and worked zealously for about 50 years in the local church, which was the mother of all the communities of the Far East Evangelical Christian-Baptist brotherhood.

In 1930, as a consequence of the arrest of my father, Peter Vins, who served as pastor of the Blagoveshchensk church from 1927-30, Georgi Shipkov once more took upon himself a responsible ministry as pastor, which lasted until 1937.

These years were especially hard for our whole brotherhood. The prayer house in Blagoveshchensk, built by the believers' own hands as long ago as 1910, was confiscated in 1930, and many preachers of the Gospel were forced into exile or were locked up in prisons. Georgi Shipkov was almost the only one left of the ministers of the church in Blagoveshchensk.

Under the influence of persecution in these years there began to appear among the believers those who were faint hearted, fearful, and even time-servers. Fallen and broken officers of the church emerged, and it was from these that the authorities began in subsequent years to form religious groupings obedient to atheism.

The majority of believers, however, courageously continued to serve God.

In 1938 Georgi Shipkov was sent to Omsk. He settled down in a small room in a house belonging to believers. He was physically very weak. But the secret police did not leave him in peace: they often summoned him to interrogations and threatened

131

him with a new exile farther north, in the tundra.

I saw Georgi Shipkov once in Omsk in 1939. He was a short, thin old man with a pointed beard, very affectionate and kind, who laid his small hand on my head and asked about my father.

In the last years of his life (1934-39) Georgi Shipkov did a great deal of work on the interpretation of the New Testament. His work was contained in a large manuscript book. Unfortunately, the fate of this material is unknown. Perhaps it is intact and is lying around somewhere unused? Perhaps believers are preserving letters, articles and other manuscript legacies of dear Georgi Shipkov? I beg the Lord to rouse the hearts of believers to seek out the precious spiritual heritage of our heroes of the faith, so that it may become the property of our whole Evangelical-Baptist brotherhood.

As an aged man, committed to the Lord to the end, Shipkov ended his earthly journey in prison.

From 1934-35 there was a lively correspondence between my father and Georgi Shipkov. Unfortunately only a small number of Shipkov's letters have been preserved.

Four of his letters are included in the present collection: one letter to my father from the Blagoveshchensk church (written by Shipkov at the commission of the church), and three personal letters from Shipkov (only a small part of the third letter has been preserved).

January 7, 1934
BLAGOVESHCHENSK

My greatly respected and warmly beloved brother in the Lord, Peter Yakovlevich, peace to you!

132

We listened to your letter of December 6, 1933, to our community at our members' meeting on January 1, 1934. By this letter we express to you our most lively gratitude for remembering us and for your exhortations. We have always prayed and will continue to pray for you, that the God and Father of our Lord Jesus Christ will grant you the power of endurance to bear to the end the cross of affliction laid on you by the hand of God's foresight, together with the bitterness of separation and the many deprivations on the path trodden by Christ, the apostles and the martyrs. This is the path trodden by our Savior and Lord and marked out by Him for His followers for all ages (John 15: 18-20; Acts 14: 22; II Tim. 3: 12). "Suffering produces endurance, and endurance produces character, and character produces hope" (Rom. 5: 3, 4). The righteous man and witness of God in the Old Testament, tried and tested by afflictions, clothed in patience, enriched by experience, and inspired with hope, after a whole series of perplexities regarding the way of the Lord, finally says to the Lord: "I know, O Lord, that the way of man is not in himself, that it is not in man who walks to direct his steps" (Jer. 10: 23). In even more ancient, precovenant times something similar happened with another righteous man and sufferer for the Lord, who at the end of a very long series of questions with allusions to the imaginary injustice of God, bordering on open grumbling, finally said to God: "I know that thou canst do all things, and that no purpose of thine can be thwarted. 'Who is this that hides counsel without knowledge?' Therefore I have uttered what I did not understand . . . . I had heard of thee by the hearing of the ear, but now my eye sees thee; therefore I despise

133

myself, and repent in dust and ashes" (Job 42: 1-6).

"You also be patient. Establish your hearts, for the coming of the Lord is at hand . . . . As an example of suffering and patience . . . take the prophets who spoke in the name of the Lord. Behold, we call those happy who were steadfast. You have heard of the steadfastness of Job, and you have seen the purpose of the Lord, how the Lord is compassionate and merciful" (James 5: 8, 10, 11).

You, my dear and much-beloved brother, write: "Although materially we sometimes feel need, we are cheerful in spirit and thank the Lord for everything." We rejoice heartily at this spiritual cheerfulness and sincerely share your grief over material need. "Rejoice always, pray constantly, give thanks in all circumstances" (I Thess. 5: 16-18)—such is the threefold principle of Christians in your position.

Praise Christ, brother, for our joy!
Praise Christ, brother, for the
    cup of suffering!
The King of Heaven Himself is coming to us
And He is bringing us bliss.
For eternity is already quite near!

from *Hymns of Faith*

For each of us, however, who is not in your position, there is another urgent, unremitting principle: "Let him who is taught the word share all good things with him who teaches" (Gal. 6: 6). And we have tried to put it into practice, although not to the measure we would wish, but to the measure that is possible for us—the minimum. If we have not

134

thought about this earlier, then it was as a consequence of a question that troubled us: should our meetings take place in the cooperative-association house, or will we, according to the example of the Molokans, have to close them because of the absence of resources to pay for the premises (165 rubles a month, not counting maintenance expenses)? You can easily imagine what would happen to us, as an organizational unit, (which for the second winter now has in its care children abandoned at the will of fate by their fathers), if we, as a community, closed down our meetings and thus disbanded ourselves as an organization!

In general one may say: if we abandoned our meetings, then our community would lose its identity and disperse. But having had "the help that comes from God" (Acts 26: 22), we stand firm to this day, witnessing with conviction to the truth and openly preaching Christ in our meetings. The help from God consisted of this, that He instilled into us an awareness of the danger that threatened us—to scatter to our homes—and the intention of upholding His work at any price. For the latter it was necessary for us to make desperate efforts to gather material resources, and only thanks to the voluntary and generous response of some members of the community did we emerge from this tight corner. "I thank him who has given me strength for this, Christ Jesus our Lord" (I Tim. 1: 12). In the future we are faced in this respect with the prospect of walking along the path of our creed by forced marches, as they are called in military terms. We profoundly believe and hope that He who gave us power in the past until this day will also give it to us in the future,

135

for He is "the same yesterday and today and for ever" (Heb. 13: 8).

Today we are celebrating a double festival: the day of the resurrection from the dead of our Lord Jesus Christ and the day of His birth into the world by the Old Style [calendar] (so this is our second Christmas). We are sending to you the material fruit of our meetings today. Accept it as an expression of our powerful love to you.

In conclusion, from my heart I wish you, as I wish myself, a joyful meeting, and that you may stay together without parting for an instant in the coming year. I pray to the All-merciful God for this, and I greet you in absence, dear brother Peter Yakovlevich and esteemed sister Lidia Mikhailovna. We remain unfailingly loving you in Christ Jesus, your brothers and sisters in faith, hope and love—the members of the Blagoveshchensk Baptist community.

> For the community
> and by its commission:
> G. Shipkov

"I . . . the writer of this letter, greet you in the Lord" (Rom. 16: 22).

First Letter

February 10, 1934
BLAGOVESHCHENSK
OKTYABRSKAYA STREET 102

Dear and esteemed Peter Yakovlevich,

I was very glad to receive your postcard from Novosibirsk dated January 17 this year, which M. A.

136

Zharikova passed on to me on the 6th of this month at an evening meeting. When I had read the postcard, I also read it at the conclusion of the meeting to those who were with me that evening. Everyone rejoiced and gave thanks to Him who made it possible for you to receive a passport and move to a flourishing town in Siberia from unprepossessing Biisk. We also rejoiced because M. A. informed us that the same day she had received a telegram from Lidia Mikhailovna about her move to Novosibirsk. From your postcard and Lidia Mikhailovna's telegram we concluded that you have managed to find work in your new place. From the bottom of our hearts we wish you success in your new home and at your new work. We hope that your outward situation will improve gradually; and as for your inward state we can only rejoice and thank Him who has given us strength.

Doubtless Lidia Mikhailovna has told you about our life, but not everything. After she had left for Biisk, our co-tenants of the cooperative association house were thrown out—and now we are left alone in the building and pay its rent in full (160 rubles a month), as was provided in the contract. Moreover, this winter we have been extremely harassed by lack of fuel, in spite of the legacy and consequences of the reconstruction which has taken place in past years. We have to worry about all this and exert every effort, since at the beginning of the autumn Hamlet's question stood before us: "To be or not to be?" But thanks be to Him who gave us strength: we are! We hope that in the future also we *shall be,* and, as you know, hope does not disappoint us. However, our co-tenants in the building have condemned themselves to sitting quietly at home.

As a matter of interest, where has V. P. Stepanov gone? V. N. Pertsev has gone on the advice of his doctors to Kislovodsk for treatment for aneurism (dilation of the heart) and after his return from there he stopped in Omsk. At present he is in Khabarovsk. We still don't know what his state of health is.

In conclusion I send you and our esteemed Lidia Mikhailovna . . . from myself and those who are with me . . . a greeting of love and respect.

A. F. and A. S. Zhbanov are in Omsk at the moment, since their passports have been taken away.

> Your sincerely loving:
> G. Shipkov

Second Letter

June 15, 1935
BLAGOVESHCHENSK
OKTYABRSKAYA STREET 102

Dear and greatly respected Peter Yakovlevich, peace to you!

Your kind letter of May 20, 1935, reached me in good time some while ago. I am very grateful to you for remembering me, for paying attention to me, and for your correspondence with me.

From May 12, having rented from one of our members half a house not far from Amur and Zeya for the summer season, we have begun to meet in it twice on Sundays and in the evenings of free days. I shall not say how long I had to petition the local authorities for its permission to hold meetings somewhere in the town.

How dear to me is communion
With the saints on earth.
But even this delight
Has become impossible for me.

Times change and we change with them: so said
the ancient Romans. Times change in *circumstances*
and people change in *feelings*.

When David the shepherd had no other care but
to watch over the flock of his father Jesse in
meadows green with grain and speckled with every
kind of flower, with the bright sun shining in the
cloudless sky and the gleam of the "quiet waters" in
the streams and lakes, when he had with him
whenever he moved or halted his vial of oil in his
pocket and his food for the day, so that his young
head was anointed with oil, he was provided with a
delicious meal in the fields, and his cup was overflowing—then he was inspired to utter the 23rd
psalm, calling God his Shepherd and he himself, His
sheep who was in need of nothing. When the "valley
of the shadow of death" was still far distant from
David, he said optimistically and with conviction to
his invisible but almighty Shepherd: "Even though I
walk through the valley of the shadow of death, I fear
no evil; for thou art with me; thy rod and thy staff,
they comfort me." But when David became a man
and was faced with being the shepherd not of the
sheep of Jesse, his earthly father, but of the people of
Jehovah, his heavenly father, who first of all had led
him through "the valley of the shadow of death"
(not the valley of death, but the valley of its *shadow*),
his bold confidence changed to gloomy pessimism
and his joyful hymn of praise was rearranged into a

sorrowful song of prayer. Then the "shadow of death," taking on human form, threatened David and he prayed to His Leader: "Be gracious to me, O God, for men trample upon me . . . my enemies trample upon me all day long," then this shadow took on the form of lions, and the sheep of the Lord complained to his Shepherd: "I lie in the midst of lions . . . their teeth are spears and arrows, their tongues sharp swords." Then this shadow of fatal danger altered to an engulfing bog and he wailed to his Savior: "Save me, O God! For the waters have come up to my neck. I sink in deep mire, where there is no foothold" (Psalm 56: 1, 2; 57: 4; 69: 1, 2).

Only after he had passed believing and hoping through the "valley of the shadow of death" could he sing the hymn of praise to his Deliverer, Savior and Lord: "I waited patiently for the Lord; he inclined to me and heard my cry. He drew me up from the desolate pit, out of the miry bog, and set my feet upon a rock, making my steps secure. He put a new song in my mouth, a song of praise to our God" (Psalm 40: 1-3). Only then does the theoretical human confidence: "I fear no evil; for thou art with me," become divine, practical fact: "He is at my right hand that I may not be shaken" (Acts 2: 25).

So it is with all positive and decisive travelers "into the paradise of Canaan, where is the dawn of eternal happiness." So it was with David, Christ's forefather in the flesh, and with all righteous men. So it was with David's descendants in the natural human way, the root of David which God created, and with the God-Man Jesus Christ (Rev. 22: 16). "In the days of his flesh" (Heb. 5: 7), He more than once and in different ways told His disciples about the purpose of His incarnation or taking on human form, which consisted of His expiatory, sacrificial death. He looked on His human flesh as a sacrifice, but His divinity represented an eternal Priest in the strength of the uniqueness of His sacrifice. Posing or appearing as "the great shepherd of the sheep, by the blood of the eternal covenant" (Heb. 13: 20), He announced to His unbelieving hearers: "I am the good shepherd . . . and I lay down my life for the sheep . . . No one takes it from me, but I lay it down of my own accord. I have power to lay it down, and I have power to take it again" (John 10: 14, 15, 18).

Willingness for self-sacrifice and the assertion of all-powerfulness to raise himself from the dead . . . . In another instance, declaring to His disciples His eternal priesthood and His sacrifice, universal in its application, ageless throughout time and all-sufficient in its strength, He said: "The Son of man came not to be served but to serve, and to give his life as a ransom for many" (Mt. 20: 28). Such was the declaration of the God-Man Christ Jesus to both His enemies and His friends when His sacrificed, mortal half was still in complete safety, when the decisive, not merely critical but shattering moment approached, the moment of the entry of the immortal Priest and the mortal sacrifice in one Person no longer into the "valley of the shadow of death," but into the gates of death itself—shameful, terrible, torturing death. He said this when the rope of necessity, thrown onto the neck of the sacrifice, dragged it irresistibly to the place of slaughter. Then the sacrifice, mortally afflicted in soul, His body trembling terribly in a cold sweat, mingled with blood, on a bitterly cold night in early spring, "with loud cries and tears"

141

(Heb. 5: 7) prayed to His Heavenly Father for mercy, saying: "My Father, if it be possible, let this cup pass from me." But the strong-willed Priest said to the Almighty: "Thy will be done" (Mt. 26: 39, 42). The unshakable resolution of the divine Priest overcame the fear of the trembling human sacrifice—and our redemption was accomplished.

As regards the general redemption of each and every one who wishes for himself salvation from the power of sin and eternal death, one can say in the words of a verse from a psalm: "Death is annulled and we are delivered." In certain cases, however, after bitter experiences endured in the "valley of the shadow of death" for Christ's sake, after coming out from it "tried in the crucible of misfortunes and afflictions of this life," instead of the one verse just quoted from the psalm one can sing with delight the whole 124th psalm as a hymn of praise to the Leader and Deliverer and as a triumphal song of victory in Christ after gaining a glorious victory over evil "through him who loved us" (Rom. 8: 37).

You, dear Peter Yakovlevich, like other brothers confessing the faith who have passed through "the valley of the shadow of death" under the leadership and protection of Him who "died, and behold I am alive for evermore" (Rev. 1: 18), and to whom from the moment of His glorious resurrection from the dead, now and for evermore is given "all authority in heaven and on earth" (Mt. 28: 18), from personal experience can bear testimony better than all of us who have not passed through to the truth of the words of Psalm 22: 4 and Matthew 28: 18.

I understand from your letter that I. I. Bondarenko and V. I. Kolesnikov have been overtaken by the same illness as our Sasha. Did I understand you correctly? Sasha's situation is the same as before. The crisis of the illness cannot yet be seen and lies before us.

I close with greetings to you, to our esteemed Lidia Mikhailovna and little Georgi, to S. V. Petrov and all the dear ones in the blood of Christ and the Spirit of the living God. Pray for us.

> With sincere affection
> and respect:
> G. Shipkov

P. S. Where are V. N. Pertsev and his family now?

Third Letter (Fragment)

"God helps those who help themselves." This is not an irreligious but a *godly* proverb. However, people are bitterly disillusioned about swift help from God and usually first fall into despair and then into godlessness. In this way their faith, like a spark from a crucible, first of all soars gleaming upward to the heavens, then is extinguished in the night air and falls as a speck of dust to the cold earth. Alas for such "believers"!

This is not the kind of faith in God and the kind of hope in his all-powerfulness and mercy that true Christians and reborn children of God should have. The central pillar in the church of God's grace looks on the trial of believers by afflictions as a purifying fire, melting gold to give it greater value (I Peter 1: 3-7). Gold in the smelting furnace is not destroyed, but is purified and gains in value. True faith is subject to the same process and attains the same result in the crucible of trial by afflictions. Another pillar of the same church orders believers to have not a simple but a "great joy" when they fall into "various trials," for the "testing of their faith," leading to an increase of steadfastness, which has its full effect on those who are tried (James 1: 2-4). And finally, the third pillar of the Gentile section of the same church reasons that the gift of God we have received, faith, with its accompanying afflictions, evolves, not decreasing, but increasing in new experiences and raising itself by degrees higher and higher to the faultless sensation of the love of God, poured out in the hearts of believers by the Holy Spirit given to them in the day they turn to the Lord (Rom. 5: 1-5). On the basis of such an experience, the apostle asks: "Who shall separate us from the love of Christ? Shall tribulation, or distress, or persecution, or famine, or nakedness, or peril, or sword?" And at once he answers with complete conviction: "I am sure that neither death, nor life, nor angels (fallen), nor principalities (those in command), nor things present, nor things to come, nor powers (authorities), nor height (worldly position), nor depth (humiliation in the world), nor anything else in all creation, will be able to separate us from the love of God in Christ Jesus our Lord" (Rom. 8: 35-39).

From the very beginning of Christianity to us believers "it has been granted to you that for the sake of Christ you should not only believe in him but also suffer for his sake" (Phil. 1: 29). His redemptive sufferings for believers must necessarily be compensated for by their sufferings in thanks to Him. As in the Old Testament . . . .

LOOKING TO JESUS[4]

Therefore, since we are surrounded by so great a cloud of witnesses, let us also lay aside every weight, and sin which clings so closely, and let us run with perseverance the race that is set before us, looking to Jesus the pioneer and perfecter of our faith.

Hebrews 12: 1, 2.

In ancient times in the heathen world there were popular festivals among the Greeks which were called the Olympic Games. These holy festivals were held once every four years, and at the approach of every Olympic Game all quarrels among the Hellenic peoples ceased, and all of Greece gathered on the Olympic plain for the festival of the games. Among other games there was the foot-race. Those who wanted to run in the race had to go through a nine-month course to prepare themselves for it.

For this purpose the Greeks had special schools called *gymnasia*. In these schools those preparing to run in the race to receive the prize refrained from food, as far as possible, so that their bodies would be lighter. When they practiced they ran completely naked, so that nothing would restrict their movements.

These schools received their name *gymnasia* because it comes from the word *gymnos,* meaning "naked." Therefore Paul writes in another of his letters: "Do you not know that in a race . . . every athlete exercises self-control in all things . . . to receive

---

[4]A sermon of G. I. Shipkov, issued by the publishing house Raduga (rainbow).

a perishable wreath" (I Cor. 9: 24, 25), and here he advises "lay aside every weight" so that it will be easier to run the race or the course. The race or course was the name of a level, smooth place, sprinkled with sand, so that no one would injure himself by a fall or hurt his foot running. At the end of the race was set a chain, near which the judge sat in state in a high place and gave out prizes to the victors in the race. The winner of the race was rewarded with a crown woven of olive leaves. To receive this was regarded as a great honor for a man. Then the crowned victor was chaired through the streets of the nearest town to the joyful shouts of countless numbers of triumphant people who had witnessed the races and the victories. Then when the victor returned to his own town, for his triumphal entry a breach was made in the town wall, which signified that the town, being honored to have such a valiant citizen, had no need of walls for its defense.

Poets immortalized the name of the victorious hero in their verses, and in the next popular festivals and games the places of honor were taken by the victors of previous competitions.

This is the kind of race Paul had in mind for comparison when he wrote these lines to the Hebrew Christians, who were familiar with the heathen games. "Since we are surrounded by so great a cloud of witnesses," he said, "let us also lay aside every weight, and sin which clings so closely, and let us run with perseverance the race that is set before us, looking to Jesus the pioneer and perfecter of our faith."

Let us dwell on these words and meditate on their meaning. This will lead us to the following:

The significance of:

146

1. Every weight and sin which clings so closely,
2. The race that is set before us,
3. Looking to Jesus, and
4. The cloud of witnesses.

1. *"Let us also lay aside every weight."*

Every passion and evil lust, every unlawful desire or excessive devotion to something earthly—unnecessary care for the flesh, accumulation of wealth, winning honor and fame from this world, and similar things—all these can be a burden on the shoulders of a Christian, can trouble him on the way of his Christian calling, force him to bow his back just when he should walk straight with his head held high. These things can drag and crush him down to the ground just when his purpose and aim is to strive upward toward the heights of Heaven, to Almighty God.

Such a burden often presses a Christian down to the ground and plunges him in the dust, where he grovels like a worm, when he should be soaring in the heavens like an eagle. Our Lord likens such a burden—thought and worry about worldly things—to thorns which choke the good seed of the Gospel which has been sown. "As for what was sown among thorns," He explained the parable to His disciples, "this is he who hears the word, but the cares of the world and the delight in riches choke the word, and it proves unfruitful" (Mt. 13: 22).

Care for this life and the seduction of wealth have their power not only over those who hear the word, but also over those who have accepted it. Therefore Paul reminds the Colossian Christians of the task lying before them with the words: "Set your minds on things that are above" (Col. 3: 2).

He saw that thought about worldly things (which he otherwise refers to as care for the flesh), if it is not halted and contained within the limits of the necessary, will degenerate into lust. "Many, of whom I have often told you and now tell you even with tears, live as enemies of the cross of Christ. Their end is destruction, their god is the belly, and they glory in their shame, with minds set on earthly things" he wrote in his letter to the Philippians (3: 18, 19).

As you see, preoccupation and excessive worry about earthly things can mean destruction for a Christian, and so our Lord, forewarning His disciples concerning the suddenness of His coming, said: "But take heed to yourselves lest your hearts be weighed down with dissipation and drunkenness and cares of this life" (Lk. 21: 34).

A Christian can first become attached to something earthly unconsciously, then begin to love the world, and then be absorbed by it. In America there is a plant which catches flies. This plant looks like other plants; there is nothing special about it. The fly lands on it and walks along its leaf, but the moment it touches the sensitive filament with which each leaf of the plant is provided, the leaf springs shut in an instant, like a trap, and remains closed until it has sucked all the juices out of the fly, leaving only dust. So it is with the Christian. First he can fall into the clutches of this world, then lose the power of his spiritual life, and finally become a cast-off.

A burden in this world, apart from "the lust of the flesh and the lust of the eyes" is also the "pride of life" (I John 2: 16), which adheres to a man and can weigh down and crush a Christian even worse than the former lusts.

A man who has once confessed Christ can subsequently grow conceited before his brothers in the faith because of his worldly advantages: status, education, rights, title, and so on, which even for the most sincere and humble Christian may become at times a hindrance in the race of spiritual wholesomeness, forcing him to straighten his back where it is least of all needed, or to bend it where this is quite unnecessary.

A weight attached to a person forces him to do both things. Paul, who ordered Christians to throw off every weight, serves for us as a noble example of a free zealot. After he had turned to Christ, he considered all the advantages given to him by his birth and education—learning, honor, fame, and similar things—as vanity, as refuse for the sake of the superiority of knowing Christ Jesus, so that at the end of his life, summing up the result under all the varied and numerous experiences of the race he had run, he cried out joyfully: "I have fought the good fight, I have finished the race, I have kept the faith. Henceforth there is laid up for me the crown of righteousness, which the Lord, the righteous judge, will award to me on that Day" (II Tim. 4: 7, 8).

As well as a weight from above, a Christian can have an obstacle below, which here is called "sin which clings so closely." In literal translation it would be "tight and closely fitting sin," that is sin (i.e., base feeling) which like long, tight clothing, enfolding a man all around, forces him to stumble frequently, and so encumbers the swiftness of his movements.

Confessing Christ can free one from the old man, but it can leave with a person some particular weak-

149

ness which is pardonable in his eyes, like a jersey worn next to the skin, which will squeeze his chest as he runs the race of life, and finally suffocate him.

If this particular weakness is not restrained and crushed in time, it can degenerate into a beloved sin, and then it will be so hard for a man to free himself of it! He will have to uproot it from himself, but how?

Our Lord compares this uprooting with cutting off one's own right arm and plucking out one's own right eye.

2. *"Let us run with perseverance the race that is set before us."*

Christians have before them a race which must be run, a race of service and suffering, a path of active and suffering obedience to God. This race is charted by the will and counsel of God and marked by the glorious footprints of faithful servants of God who ran this race in their time and rested from their labors. Consequently the goal toward which he must run, and the prizes which the judge will award, are already known to the Christian. This race can be run only with endurance and constancy. Endurance is necessary to meet difficulties on the Christian way; and in order not to be left behind by others and be led astray, constancy in faith is required.

Endurance and faith are the triumphant forces by which alone it is possible to defeat the world and enter into victorious glory. "By your endurance you will gain your lives," said the Lord Jesus (Lk. 21: 19).

"Suffering produces endurance, and endurance produces character, and character produces hope, and hope does not disappoint us" (Rom. 5: 3-5). For you have need of endurance, so that you may do the will of God and receive what is promised (Heb. 10: 36).

This is the victory that overcomes the world, our faith. Who is it that overcomes the world but he who believes that Jesus is the Son of God? (I John 5: 4, 5).

Such is the strength of gracious faith.

3. *"Looking to Jesus, the pioneer and perfecter of our faith."*

In the previous chapter of this letter, Paul set out a long list of Old Testament saints who had borne testimony by their faith. They can give us a model of faith and an example of endurance. However, the apostle does not point them out to be imitated. Not surprisingly, he had before him a better model for imitation than the holy men he had listed, who, even though they had been justified and saved by the mercy of God, nonetheless had in their lives failings and vices, although these were covered and forgiven by God. Paul sets here as an example for imitation the unblemished and pure Lamb of God, the Son of Man "the man Christ Jesus," in whom there was no sin at any time in His life, who could boldly throw to His enemies the challenge: "Which of you convicts me of sin?" (John 8: 46), and in whom dwelt the fullness of human perfections.

"Looking to Jesus, the pioneer and perfecter of our faith," says Paul; looking to Him who began and perfected our faith. He began it when, laying the

151

foundation of faith in the restoration of the fallen race of Adam, He said to His Father: "Lo, I have come to do thy will, O God" (Heb. 10: 7), and He perfected it when this restoration was completed by Him on the Cross in all its foretold and expected fullness and He cried, "It is finished" (John 19: 30).

As I have already said, Christians have before them a race of service and suffering. As in service, so in suffering, we shall always look to Jesus, for He both performed service and endured suffering.

My beloved brothers and sisters! We are called to the Lord's service. Each of us is placed in the Christian race not so that we can stand there idly, but so that we can go forward, doing the work of the Lord. Each of us has both his duty and his sphere of activity for the creation of the body of Christ—the Church, and each of us must take his example from Jesus. Jesus serves as an example for each and every one. Young person, brother or sister, under the guardianship and authority of your parents! Look to Jesus and learn from Him, for He is "gentle and lowly in heart" (Mt. 11: 29). In His everlasting humility, being the divine Son of the Eternal God, He was obedient to His parents in the flesh. He before whom myriads of angels bowed down in the land of immortal light, Himself bowed to the will of His earthly parents in the dark vale of life. He who was the almighty agent of the creation of the whole world, the Creator of all, whom the heaven of heavens could not contain, worked with His own hands, worn until they were calloused, as a carpenter, and was housed by day in a cramped workshop in Nazareth, and by night in the stuffy room of immigrants from Judea—Joseph and Mary. He who "upholding everything by his word of power" in His divine preaching together with His Father, opening His generous hand and showering every living thing with blessings (Ps. 145: 16), labored in the circle of an earthly family at the joiner's bench to earn His daily bread by the sweat of his brow in order to maintain and feed the family that was left in His hands: His poor mother, and the elderly Joseph, if in fact he lived until Jesus reached maturity. Our Lord lived in obedience to His earthly parents until He was thirty years old, and by the obedience which He showed them He left to children a model of perfect obedience for children.

Then we are faced by a lesson, both we who have attained manhood and the full development of our powers, and also those who have lived to a venerable old age. We, even more than children, need to look once and continue to look constantly at Jesus, the pioneer and perfecter of our faith, so that, having looked at Him with the eyes of the true faith of grace on the day we turn to Him, we shall continue to look at Him for the rest of our life afterward and by His example "work the works . . . while it is day; night comes, when no one can work" (John 9: 4).

When our Lord reached thirty years of age He entered upon the business not of His temporary parents in the flesh, but the business of His eternal Father, His divine Parent. He appeared there as the servant of God who had been foretold, ready to fulfill any and every wish of Him who had sent Him. In full obedience to the heavenly will and in the deep humility of its earthly fulfillment, our Lord went to John the Baptist, the great servant of God, but a servant of God lower than Himself; the God-man went to a man, the Creator to the created, and submitted Himself to Baptism at his hands. John the Baptist, despite his protest and his desire to be himself baptized by Jesus, all the same in fulfillment of "all righteousness" (Mt. 3: 15), baptized Jesus, the Lamb of God, in the waters of the Jordan. Let the proud in spirit then humble himself, and look to see for what and by whom was baptized the One whom you acknowledge as the Savior of the human race?

Later, after being baptized and receiving the fullness of the Holy Spirit, the Lord Jesus, knowing that He would have to withstand the temptations of the enemy, prepared for it with prayer and fasting; and when the tempter appeared, our Lord conquered him by the power of the words of God written in the Scriptures.

After this the Lord Jesus no longer went about in the desert, but through towns and villages, "doing good and healing all" (Acts 10: 38).

If we trace carefully all the actions of our Savior—the man as well as the divine actions—we shall see that on all of them is laid the ineffaceable stamp of God's mercy and compassion toward the fallen and suffering human race. The Lord Jesus one day fed five thousand men with five loaves of bread, healed the sick and the lepers just by the touch of His hand, drove out demons, and raised the dead by His word alone.

Everywhere men's needs became a part of Him, and He became intensely and sincerely involved in all human needs. He rejoiced with those who rejoiced and wept with those who wept. For example, what roused Him to go to the wedding in Cana of Galilee, where He performed His first miracle, turning the water into wine? What made Him shed tears in Bethany at the grave of Lazarus, whom He had come to resurrect? What if not sympathy for men's joy and compassion for their grief roused Him to do both these things?

In an active life of service to God, we shall look to Jesus and act as He acted. If temptation draws near to us, and the tempter seduces us with veiled suggestions toward sin, then let us drive him away from ourselves just as Jesus did, by counsel with the will of our Heavenly Father as set forth in His word. Of course, in many things we are in no position to imitate Him.

We cannot feed a great number of hungry people with five loaves, but we do have the opportunity to become involved actively in men's urgent and pressing needs, and to arouse in other people the impulse toward charity to help the hungry, the naked, and those without shelter. We cannot heal the sick, but we can make sacrifices for a hospital, for medical treatment for the sick, and for their care. We cannot raise the dead, as the Lord Jesus raised Jairus' daughter, or the only son of the poor widow, or Lazarus, so that their loved ones should not be devoured by excessive grief and need. By our active involvement, sincere compassion, and heartfelt consolation in others' misfortunes, we can wipe away whole streams of the tears of widows and orphans. In an active working life in the race of service to Christ in the person of His and our younger brothers, we must always look to Him and imitate Him.

In the second place, we are also called to suffer for the name of Christ—to take part in the sufferings of Jesus. Not all of us are assigned by God to be

155

"blessed, exiled for the truth" for Him, to drag out our existence in prisons and in exile, but each of us suffers in some measure, and on each of us, according to our strength, a cross is laid. "They persecuted me, they will persecute you," said our Lord to His disciples (John 15: 20).

Therefore suffering is characteristic of all His followers. Without mentioning beatings, prison and exile—suspicion, mockery, profanity, and that sort of thing are always the lot of true followers of Christ in this life. Therefore in our sufferings for the name of Jesus we shall always look to Him Himself, the great sufferer. If we are dishonored and defamed for confessing our faith according to the Gospel of Jesus Christ, then let us look to Jesus, the pioneer and perfecter of our faith, and we shall see what kind of dishonor and defamation this is in comparison with His dishonor and defamation. He, being through His divine nature the Lord of glory, whom numberless angels worshipped and served—through His human nature hung on a cross, naked, spat upon, crowned with thorns, and even in the last minutes of His life an abusive crowd of many people did not cease to throw at Him the sharp darts of mockery. If burning grief fills our hearts and terrible misgivings squeeze our breasts, then let us look again at Him whose grief surpassed all our griefs taken together, at Jesus, the man of sorrows, when He, the only-begotten Son of the Heavenly Father cried out so bitterly to Him: "My God, my God, why hast thou forsaken me?" (Mt. 27: 46); and before that prayed to Him in Gethsemane, thrown down to the dust in bloody sweat by the weight of the coming cross, in a struggle of mortal agony: "Father, if thou art willing, remove this cup from me; nevertheless not my will, but thine, be done" (Luke 22: 42).

If our enemies hound and tyrannize us, causing us suffering, then let us look to Hi: "He was wounded for our transgressions, he was bruised for our iniquities" (Is. 53:5). At the moment of the most cruel torture, when they were hammering nails into His hands and feet, He prayed: "Father, forgive them; for they know not what they do" (Luke 23: 34).

Finally, if death should come and lay his cold hand on one of us, let him then for the last time in his earthly life fix his gaze on the dying Lord, devoted to His Father "unto death, even death on a cross" (Phil. 2: 8), and let him say in His words: "Father, into thy hands I commit my spirit!" (Luke 23: 46).

In trials and sorrows in the race of mortal sufferings we shall look only to Jesus and imitate only Him.

4. "*Therefore, since we are surrounded by so great a cloud of witnesses.*"

As I have already said at the beginning of this talk, the Greek heroes ran their race in the presence of many witnesses—before the face of all of Greece gathered together. We Christians have even more witnesses surrounding our earthly race than those Greek athletes. We are called to run the race of life before the face of this world, no—before the face of the whole universe gathered together—the face of Heaven and earth. "We have become a spectacle to the world, to angels and to men," said Paul (I Cor. 4: 9). That is how many witnesses we have! Men look at us, some critically, with hostility, wishing to criti-

157

cize our every action, but others questioningly, with curiosity, wishing to know if we are really Christians and children of God, while their dark souls are thirsting for spiritual light, which should shine from our faith and disperse the gloom of the perishing world. We Christians are light, and everyone looks at the light. We are the characters on the stage of life, and everyone looks at us, both from low places and from the highest circles. We are also watched with avid curiosity from the celestial world.

We are watched by those who in their time also ran the race that was set before them—"the spirits of just men made perfect" and who now form a "festal assembly" and "the assembly of the first-born who are enrolled in heaven" (Heb. 12: 23). We are watched with increasing attention by the angels, stooping downward and ready to bear the victor with joy on their arms and to carry him in triumph through radiant streets to the heavenly city, to the bosom of the Lord and Father of all, as once they bore Lazarus to Abraham's bosom. We are watched with everlasting tenderness by the pioneer and perfecter of our faith Himself, He who is the Judge and the distributor of the prizes—our Lord Jesus, who holds in His outstretched hand the victor's crown and says to each one of us: "Conquer!" "He who conquers, I will grant him to sit with me on my throne . . . Be faithful unto death, and I will give you the crown of life" (Rev. 3: 21; 2: 10).

We are watched with unfathomable love by the Lord of everything and everyone—the God and Father of our Lord Jesus Christ.

6

Nikolai Odintsov

1870 - ??

"Remember your leaders, those who spoke to you the word of God; consider the outcome of their life, and imitate their faith" (Heb. 13: 7).

"I anticipate a great spiritual awakening of my own people, a broad and deep reformation movement in our vast land that is so rich in opportunities. I hear the approach of Him who is coming to us from the heavens in the fullness of His glory and with a joyfully beating heart I turn to Him and pray fervently: "Come, Lord Jesus!"

Thus wrote Nikolai Odintsov, in the journal *The Baptist,* No. 1, 1927, as he was praying and anticipating a great spiritual awakening in our land.

For many years now the believers of our brotherhood have remembered Nikolai Odintsov with great warmth and love, and with great respect. Many who knew him personally bear witness that he was a very modest and simple brother, sympathetic, thoughtful and attentive to everyone.

His brother ministers emphasize Odintsov's extreme adherence to principle in matters of faith, his faithfulness to evangelical teaching, his courage and steadfastness in the defense of preaching, and the absence of any inclinations at all to compromise with unbelief.

The Lord placed him to serve in a most responsible post at one of the most difficult periods of the history of our Evangelical-Baptist brotherhood.

Odintsov did not yield, did not retreat, in no way betrayed the work of God.

He remained to the end in the high position of Chairman of the Christian-Baptist Union, until the very day of his arrest in 1933, and shared the full burden of persecution for the faith with the entire brotherhood. Nikolai Odintsov died as a martyr.

For the generation of young people who came into the church in the war years and in the first years after the war, Nikolai Odintsov and his comrades in the ministry were examples to be imitated.

Years passed by . . . More and more new generations of believers come into the Church. For many young Christians the name Nikolai Odintsov was buried far away in the depths of time.

The leadership of the All-Union Council buried in oblivion the names of faithful servants of God who had died in the camps. And it was forbidden even to pray for those who were still languishing in prison.

Recorded in old Christian journals, which have become a great rarity after innumerable arrests and searches, the ministry of Odintsov and other brothers came to an abrupt end in 1928, and what happened later was passed on only by word of mouth, under one's breath . . .

Nikolai Odintsov was born on December 8, 1870. Three years before his birth Nikita Isaevich Voronin, the pioneer of the Evangelical-Baptist brotherhood in Russia, turned to the Lord and received the baptism of faith. A living torrent of evangelical teaching began to flow across the plains of Russia, drawing into its ranks all those who were thirsting for salvation and eternal life.

The news of the Gospel reached Nikolai Odintsov also. He turned to the Lord as a young man of twenty. In Christ he found salvation and the meaning of life.

In 1891 Odintsov entered into an eternal covenant with the Lord through baptism by immersion. The baptism was performed in the Volga in Saratov district. The heavens and the waters of the Russian river heard his vow to serve the Lord in good conscience. Odintsov kept his vow. He dedicated his life to witnessing for Christ, up to his martyr's death.

Nikolai Odintsov was the first living stone set by God in the house-building of the Saratov Evangelical Christian-Baptist Church. It was there also that his preaching ministry began.

In 1909 Odintsov was ordained to the ministry of preaching. He was ordained by brother V.V. Ivanov-Klyshnikov, together with brothers D.I. Mazaev, S.P. Stepanov, and V.P. Stepanov. After his ordination, Odintsov visited many communities of our brotherhood. He preached in the towns and villages of Povolzhe and the Caucasus, in Moscow and Petersburg, and everywhere his spiritual labor was accompanied by abundant spiritual blessings from the Lord.

In 1913 he made his first visit to the most distant

region of Russia—the Far East. The believers of the Far East were cut off from the whole Evangelical Christian-Baptist brotherhood because of the great distances and the constant shortage of itinerant preachers. Every visit to their region by brothers from central Russia brought them great encouragement and strength in the faith.

After 1917 Nikolai Odintsov took a most active part in the publishing of Christian journals, pamphlets, and books, and was blessed in his work in the Moscow Evangelical Christian-Baptist Church.

On December 15, 1924, the Plenum of the All-Union Council of Baptists took place in Moscow, at which Ilya Andreevich Golyaev was elected chairman of the council and Odintsov assistant and treasurer. The newly elected council in the person of its chairman defined its main task thus:

> As I enter into such a responsible position before the Lord, in the strength of our Lord's command: "Go into all the world and preach the gospel to the whole creation" (Mark 16: 15), I set as my chief task, the directing of all my abilities and all our united resources to the work of mission. This was the mandate given to me by the Plenum of the Council of our Fraternal Union in accordance with the will of God (*The Baptist*, No. 2, 1925, p.l.).

In January 1925, after a seven-year break, publication of *The Baptist* was renewed, and from the fourth issue Odintsov was its editor.

In 1926 there began a particularly responsible period in Nikolai Odintsov's life and ministry. At the

26th Baptist Congress in Moscow in 1926 Odintsov was elected chairman of the Federal Baptist Union. In these years he was constantly delivering sermons about Christ, lecturing on Bible courses in Moscow, and making trips to conferences and congresses of the vast Evangelical Christian-Baptist brotherhood in our country. He took part in the work of conferences and congresses in Siberia, the Far East, Central Asia, Povolzhe, the Ukraine, and also the fourth World Baptist Congress in Toronto in 1928.

During his visits to Evangelical Christian-Baptist churches in different parts of our country, Odintsov attached great importance to conversations about the basic principles of Evangelical Christians Baptists.

His aim was that all the brotherhood should have a profound mastery of the basic principles of our doctrine and that they should be widely disseminated; for in these principles is concentrated the fundamental Gospel truth of the apostolic church—the preaching church, the missionary church.

In 1929, the forces of atheism attacked the work of the Gospel in our country.

In the summer of 1929 the journal *The Baptist* was closed down. Only seven issues of the journal came out in 1929. In autumn of the same year the Bible courses were stopped. Students who had arrived to begin their studies went sadly back home.

On the brink of the impending persecution, Odintsov wrote the article "A model for the faithful," which was published in the second issue of *The Baptist* in 1929.

In this article, which was dedicated to the selfless servant of God, Vasily Ivanov-Klyshnikov, who remained faithful to God through the persecutions of the Tsarist regime, Odintsov was preparing the Evangelical Christian-Baptist brotherhood for new trials for the faith.

In this article Odintsov wrote: "Looking to the Author and Finisher of our faith, Ivanov-Klyshnikov always performed the exalted work of a servant of the Lord joyfully and with deep humility, despite the deprivations and trials connected with this work, the defamation and unjust gossip, the constraint and persecution."

More than once he had to convince himself in practice that "we are regarded as sheep to be slaughtered" (Rom. 8: 36), and that "it has been granted to you that for the sake of Christ you should not only believe in him but also suffer for his sake" (Phil. 1: 29), and he was not "surprised at the fiery ordeal, which comes upon you to prove you, as though something strange were happening to you" (I Peter 4: 12), remaining unshakable in affliction in the recognition "that this is to be our lot" (I Thess. 3: 3).

In 1929 Odintsov's closest assistant, the Secretary of the Federal Baptist Union, Pavel Ivanov-Klyshnikov, the son of the above mentioned Vasily Vasilievich, was arrested and sent off to Kazakhstan.

In the same year the authorities closed down the Baptist Union itself. It is true that in 1930 this leading Baptist body renewed its activity, but then it was on a federal basis, since the authorities had dissolved the local Baptist Unions. Although the Union's fraternal center had resumed its work, it had no printing organ or itinerant preachers.

In May 1930 the secret police confiscated a house in Moscow, at 29 Brestskaya Street, which belonged to the Baptist Union. It housed Bible courses, the offices of the Union, and the living quarters of the workers of the Union's administration: Odintsov, Datsko, Ivanov-Klyshnikov.

All these years Nikolai Odintsov made a courageous stand for the work of God in our land and to the end remained faithful to his calling and his election. He struck no bargains with atheism.

Nikolai Odintsov realized that soon he would face separation from his nearest and dearest, from his friends in the faith and in service. At that time thousands of brothers were already languishing in exile, in prisons and in camps for the faith of Christ. Odintsov encouraged the believers, calling them to courage and faithfulness to the Lord to the very end. According to the example of the apostle Paul he would say to his close friends: ". . . imprisonment and afflictions await me. But I do not account my life of any value nor as precious to myself, if only I may accomplish my course and the ministry which I received from the Lord Jesus, to testify to the gospel of the grace of God" (Acts 20: 23, 24).

On the night of November 5, 6, 1933, Odintsov was arrested and sentenced to three years' imprisonment. He served his term in Yaroslav prison. Alexandra Mozgova, a co-worker in the Baptist Union office, was arrested at the same time as Odintsov. She too was sentenced to three years in labor camps. Later she told how she had had a confrontation with Odintsov during the investigation.

Odintsov was led into the investigator's office. He was unshaven and his cheeks were sunken. He gave Alexandra Mozgova a friendly look and encouragement for the thorny patch which lay ahead of her.

Odintsov behaved calmly and with assurance, although physically he was very weak indeed. During the investigation itself he selflessly defended the things of God.

After his trial Nikolai Odintsov was sent to Yaroslav prison, where he was kept for the whole of his term of imprisonment. After he had served his prison sentence, he was sent into exile in Eastern Siberia. He spent his exile in the village of Makovskoye in the Krasnoyarsk district. This village is situated on the *taiga* river Ket, seventy kilometers from Yeniseisk. Makovskoye is an ancient Russian settlement which has just observed its 350th anniversary. Russian Cossack explorers founded it amid the slumbering Siberian forests. For tens of kilometers around there is not one village, only *taiga* and more *taiga*. Makovskoye is the traditional place of exile for religious people of different faiths. Odintsov was held in Makovskoye before the war, and after the war many believers served their exile there.

In 1937 Odintsov's wife Alexandra Stepanova came to see him in Makovskoye. When she returned home she told the believers that Nikolai was very weak physically but courageous in spirit. He sent greetings to his brothers and sisters, and was preparing to pass on to the eternal dwelling place of the Father. He often said to his wife: "I want to go home!"

There in Makovskoye in 1938 Odintsov was once again put under guard and taken away in an unknown direction.

Soon he died in prison.

Nikolai Odintsov's memory lives on among the whole Evangelical Christian-Baptist brotherhood.

His selfless, uncompromising service for the work of the Gospel, and his faithfulness to Christ until death are an inspiring example for many thousands of Christians.

A LETTER FROM ODINTSOV IN PRISON[5]

My dear brother in the Lord:

Peace to you and to all those who love the Lord! All of you are uncertain about me . . .

I shall not describe the terrors which the prisoners are experiencing, as that is a matter for a specialist historian or a simple honest man. I shall say only one thing: there is no terror like it! Can one imagine the bestial look of the hand-picked convoy escorts, who, making use of the right granted them, can shoot sick men who collapse and hunt down with vicious dogs the prisoner who falls on the road?

Can one become accustomed to constant, coarse, inhuman shouting flavored with the most awful, infernal swearing which lowers human dignity? Can one endure the constant, daily, tiresome, loathsome activity of the provocateurs and spies, who hang on one's every word and wrench at a prisoner's soul?

My body is tired and weak, my work for the Lord here in the camps is unbearably hard, and the repressions I suffer often hold me for long periods on my bare plank-bed, which represents my bed of ease.

My dear brother, you presented a petition for me to be set free ahead of time, for a "pardon," for my return to my family and my brothers in the faith.

[5]Printed here with significant abridgements.

You know, of course, not as a lawyer but as a preacher in God's harvest field, that I, as the least brother in the Lord, was set free forever and pardoned once and for all. As far as my return to my family is concerned, I shall await my family and our family up there in Heaven, "where we shall meet you beyond the wonderful river and there with incessant praise we shall serve Jesus . . ."

I have grown weak in body, but not in spirit. Jesus, my Lord, upholds me. I am informed about you only through hearsay. My body cannot bear the violence . . . "For I am already on the point of being sacrificed; the time of my departure has come." Nothing atheistic has adhered to me. "I have fought the good fight, I have finished the race, I have kept the faith." I have refused to betray God. "Henceforth there is laid up for me the crown of righteousness, which the Lord, the righteous judge, will award me on that Day" (II Tim. 4: 6-8). I have always avoided every injustice. With this my earthly life will be finished. Amen.

I often think that the brothers and sisters with whom I have shared joy, who were once given as gifts by the Lord God in the name of His Son, our Savior, will never see me again, and I shall not see all of you on this earth. I feel especially sad for the young people, for the servants of the Church, for all my brothers and sisters, for soon the terrors of persecution will fall upon you, and it is possible that members of families will suffer, fathers, mothers and children, and grandchildren, and wives, and husbands, and sisters, and brothers. Abuse of God and slander of the children of God will grow up, and "apostates from the Holy Covenant" will appear.

168

Their perfidiousness, cowardice, and servility to atheism will lead to betrayal and subversive activity in the Church of Christ, since both verbally and in writing they will justify atheist activity directed at the destruction of the Church.

With the help of the apostates, atheism will lead its faithful people into bodies for the control of church affairs, which with the help of slander and provocation and the exposure of people not servile to atheism, will take its slanderous fabrications to the secret police as denunciations as a result of which many servants of the Church, brothers and sisters, will suffer. Atheism will enter into an agreement with the apostates from the Holy Covenant. "He shall seduce with flattery those who violate the covenant; but the people who know their God shall stand firm and take action" (Dan. 11: 32).

The Leninist decree on the separation of the Church from the State and of the School from the Church, of January 23, 1918, was the first legislative deed to define the rights of citizens of the USSR with respect to religion. By this decree and by other deeds of law it is forbidden to publish any other laws or resolutions which could change the Leninist decree of January 23, 1918, or could limit or change freedom of conscience in our land.

In his article "Socialism and Religion," Lenin wrote: "We require that religion should be a private matter as far as the state is concerned. The state must have nothing to do with religion. Religious societies must not be connected with the state power. Religious and church societies must be completely free unions of like-minded citizens independent of the authorities."

It was a wise decision, judicious in the highest degree, which led to the creation of the Constitution of the RSFSR and its 13 articles, and also the above mentioned Decree of the Council of Peoples' Commissars of January 23, 1918, "On the separation of the Church from the State and of the School from the Church," as a result of which genuine freedom of conscience was insured in the great land of the USSR.

Soon after Lenin's death, to be precise, on April 8, 1929, the Resolution of the All-Union Central Executive Committee and the Council of Peoples' Commissars, "On Religious Associations," was published. This Resolution is not the last word in the chain of the infernal scheme of atheism to force the faithful children of the living God to their knees before the god of this world, Baal-atheism.

Many brothers and sisters of different ages, from young men to those advanced in years, are found, and will be found for the time being, in chains for faith in the God who foresees and holds everything in His power, and in Jesus, our Savior.

Pitiless in its senseless cruelty, atheism threw into prisons and camps very many brothers and sisters who were faithful to their Lord. However, those who are faithful to the Teacher, Jesus our Lord, will go forward and will not stop, because the path pointed out by the Savior is the right and sure path, and believers who love their Lord will never stand upon the path of compromise with godless atheism.

There will be apostates from the Holy Covenant. In collaboration with atheists ignorant in spiritual matters, and under their leadership, apostates will attempt to introduce division into the brotherhood.

170

They will support this division in order to justify confidence in themselves and to render what is due in gratitude for a quiet life, for the status they have received from atheism. After the apostates will rush those who do not hold truth dear, who will also crave thirstily for status and an easy life, those who, no matter whether afflictions and sufferings increase for their believing fathers and mothers, the members of their family, no matter whether afflictions and sufferings increase for the Church of Christ—for the time being they will go about their treacherous business to please atheism.

This will be how the struggle with religion in the USSR will be: in time it will turn into a shameful business in the eyes of the whole world for the leaders of this struggle, since these savagely cruel people will force the closure of prayer houses on believers and churches, they will oppress the servants of the church, and even physically torture and liquidate some brothers. They will construct a "case" as a result of biased investigations based on slander, and believers one and all will be condemned to prisons and camps. "Good publicity" about the unjust trials, the procurators and investigators, the camp and prison administrations will be spread throughout the world. All their actions will win approbation, as will those who pioneer, inspire and lead the campaign.

The legislator who was so eager to begin a cruel repression of religion that he published the resolution on religious associations did not even see the contradiction between this resolution and Lenin's Decree of January 23, 1918, and article 13 of the 1918 Constitution. If the Decree and article 13 of the Constitution granted believers a Church independent of the State and the freedom to spread their faith, then the Resolution had contrary aims: specifically, to put the church in a position of complete dependence on the atheist state, to which would be granted the absolute right of depriving believers of freedom of conscience. In its war with religion atheism will try to suppress freedom of religion by repression throughout the land.

It is also possible that conditions will be created for the Church with the intention of physically annihilating believers. Let us remember the history of martyrdom of the apostolic church of the first centuries, when the most cruel of all, the Roman Caesars, governed the people: Nero, Decius, Diocletian and others. Let us remind all our believing brothers and sisters what happened in those centuries under the rulers of Rome we have mentioned, who were also high priests of the pagan religion which held sway in the Roman Empire. The most cruel persecution of Christians occurred because of the slander of high priests and other priests of paganism.

The rulers of Rome used this persecution to pursue their aim of finally eradicating Christianity, the "sect of Christ" which was hostile to the pagan religion of the Empire.

It was announced that all the Christians in the towns and villages should appear on a stated day and hour in stated places for the offering of pagan sacrifices. They hunted out those who did not appear and applied to them the most refined tortures and slow-acting torments, at the same time forcing the believers to renounce Christ. Those who did not appear were deprived of civil rights, their property was confiscated, and their families were broken up. Christians were crucified on crosses, sewn up in the skins of animals and given like this to wild animals to be torn to pieces. They were sewn up in sacks, which were soaked in tar and set alight during the so-called people's festivals.

Christians were driven out of their homes because they gathered for prayer, but prayer houses were taken away. Christians were whipped, stoned, dragged along the ground, thrown into pits and prisons, deprived of burial, set upon by hungry, vicious, man-eating dogs. The bodies of tortured Christians lay in heaps in the streets of the towns.

The Christians of the apostolic church went out to preach the Word of God from the catacombs, hovels, and forests where the true Christians of the apostolic church would gather for prayer and to glorify the Eternal God: Their great song of faith, love, and hope has continued through the following ages and will continue to resound. It is a song of praise to the Almighty Lord God, and it speaks of and glorifies God's all-forgiveness and love to the whole of mankind. It calls man to moral purity and to sanctity. This song is sung by many people on all the continents of earth in our own times.

Several days ago during a convoy transfer, I, being one of the weakest prisoners, was unable to stand, and at that moment I heard a shout behind me and the momentary prick of something sharp in my back. Then I was thrown to the ground by a blow below my head. The next moment I heard swearing and felt two vicious dogs on top of me, snarling, trampling over me and tearing my already torn and dirty clothing. Then I felt a sharp pain below my stomach, where the dog's teeth were tearing to pieces my old, exhausted body which had suffered so much. I came to myself in the barracks, where my comrades, prisoners in the Lord, were binding up my wounds.

Within only three weeks I was led out and driven on to a convoy for work.

What else will there be? The Lord knows! Eternal glory to Him! Rejoice, dear brothers and sisters, as I REJOICE! Your brother, who to the end of his days has not forgotten you all, and may the name of our God and of His Son our Lord Jesus Christ be blessed and glorified!

Amen, Hallelujah!
(KRASNOYARSK DISTRICT)

7

Polina Skakunova

IN THE YEARS BEFORE THE WAR the blind Christian
poetess Polina Yakovlevna Skakunova was well
known to the believers of Povolzhe and Siberia.

In the 1920's Polina Yakovlevna and her husband
were literary workers and lived in Saratov. Polina
Yakovlevna was an active atheist. She traveled
through the villages of Saratov region giving atheist
lectures.

"We don't need God!" she used to say. "Man himself is the forger of his own happiness. I shall live as I
want to live!"

In 1925 Polina Yakovlevna's husband suddenly
died. This was a terrible blow for her. After the
funeral, when everyone had dispersed from the
cemetery, she returned to her husband's grave and
attempted to commit suicide. The cemetery watch-
man heard a shot at night. Some inner voice forced

him to get up, dress, and go to the place where the shot had sounded. Among the wreaths on the fresh grave he found Polina Yakovlevna covered in blood and unconscious. He called some people to help and took her to a hospital. Polina Yakovlevna had shot at her temple, but had not achieved what she desired. She survived, but damaged both her eyes with the shot and went blind.

Polina Yakovlevna gave way to despair and became embittered. In a conversation with a believer in Saratov in 1925 she said: "It has turned out that I could not live as I wanted . . . to make up for it. I shall die as I want!" She was stubborn and did not mean to live: she opened her veins, took poison, and even attempted to throw herself under a train.

But the Lord in His great love prevented her.

After some while, terribly ill and disfigured, Polina Yakovlevna became more calm. Unbelieving friends advised her to occupy herself with atheist literary work, for which she was taken several times to a prayer house of Evangelical Christians Baptists in Saratov. Making her way toward the meeting for the first time, she said: "I'll go, if only to laugh at them!" But the result was quite the opposite. The blind woman saw the spiritual beauty of Christ and believed in Him with all the strength of her sensitive soul, worn out by suffering. She repented of her former sinful life and her attempts at suicide, was baptized, and began to witness for Christ.

Polina Yakovlevna wrote a wonderful poem about her turning to the Lord and a great number of outstanding Christian verses. Before the war numerous copies were distributed to believers.

Her unbelieving friends forsook her; she was

deprived of her means of subsistence, but she did not renounce Christ.

For a while she lived in Omsk with Alexandra Semirech, who surrounded her with truly motherly love and care.

I remember Polina Yakovlevna—a thin intelligent woman with black spectacles covering empty eye sockets. In 1938 I was ill for half the winter with pneumonia. On many days Polina Yakovlevna sat at my bedside. I remember her kind hands straightening the blanket and giving me medicine. I remember her quiet voice when she read her poems about Christ to me, then a ten-year-old boy, and had heart-to-heart talks with me about Him.

In 1939 Polina Yakovlena was arrested in Omsk and did not return. She died an unknown death in prison. What danger did she represent for atheism?

A very great danger, obviously: she kindled people's hearts by her inner spiritual insight, her deep faith, and her poems about Christ.

8

Pavel Datsko

1884-1941

Jesus, Savior of my soul,
Let me cling to your breast,
Be my protector amid storms,
Do not desert me along the way!
I have no other refuge,
All I have is You alone,
Do not abandon me, weak as I am,
Amid worldly vanity.

How often we have sung this hymn with deep emotion and reverence in the presence of the Savior. This hymn not only calls us to a special intimacy with Christ; it also leads us into the sanctuary of God. This is evident from the radiant faces of those who sing it and those who listen. Who was the author of this remarkable hymn? For many long years I did not know . . . but I felt that he had to be a Christian of deep spirituality and marked poetic sensitivity.

Some years ago the Lord allowed me to learn who the author was. He was Pavel Yakovlevich Datsko.

Believers who knew him personally have the most joyful memories of him as a simple, sensitive Christian whose spirit never failed.

Pavel Datsko, a gifted preacher and a poet who drew his inspiration from above, was respected and loved by all our brotherhood, especially in the Ukraine where he labored so hard in the harvest fields of God.

Datsko was the author of many remarkable Christian poems, some of which have become hymns— "Jesus, Savior of the Soul," the Christmas carol "The Angels' Song," "Thou art my Savior," and others.

His poems were frequently printed in the journals *The Baptist* and *The Ukrainian Baptist*, but some were never published, including the long poem "Ruth."

Pavel Datsko was born on August 28, 1884, in the Ukraine, where the greater part of his life and his spiritual ministry were spent.

In May 1925 there took place in Kharkov the fourth congress of Baptists of the Ukraine, at which the All-Ukrainian Baptist Union was formed. A. P. Kostyukov was elected as chairman and Pavel Datsko as his deputy.

The position of the work of God in the Ukraine at the time of this congress was set forth in the following resolution:

Congress finds that the Baptist communities of the Ukraine are in a satisfactory condition. It has observed a numerical growth in membership, recently reaching an average of 15% per annum. (*The Baptist*, No. 4-5, pp. 2-3, 1925.)

The Congress defined the main task of the Baptist Union of the Ukraine:

Missionary activity, that is, the sending of evangelists to spread the Gospel, must be considered to be of first importance. All other forms of Christian activity must be subordinated to it, and all our attention must be concentrated on it.

In 1926 the 26th congress of Christians Baptists took place in Moscow, where Pavel Datsko was elected to the governing body of the Federal Baptist Union.

In 1927 he moved from Kharkov to Moscow, where he fulfilled the office of treasurer and deputy chairman of the Union, taught Bible courses, and worked as one of the editors of *The Baptist*.

Datsko never failed to give support to brother Odintsov in his work, especially in the difficult period of harassment and persecution which began in 1929.

In 1928 Pavel Datsko dedicated the following poem to Nikolai Odintsov on his birthday:

TO NIKOLAI ODINTSOV

Days of bygone feelings,
Expectations,
Hesitations,
Have flown away like a dream.
They have passed,
Hidden in the distance,
Only their memory is clear.

A new time has come,
Heavy labor,
And severe,
Promises fruit of peace.
Weariness,
Consolation,
Fill all the present year.

Now the time of days to come;
Which make all things possible,
Which bring once more
Blessing upon blessing.
Without doubt
Or confusion,
Brother, you must face them.

In 1929 brother Pavel Ivanov-Klyshnikov was sent into exile, and all the work of the executive secretary of the Baptist Union now fell on Pavel Datsko's shoulders.

In 1933 Odintsov was arrested. Pavel Datsko was the only one left of the older, experienced members of the leadership of the Baptist Union. In 1936 he too was sent into exile, from which he did not return until the autumn of 1938. His wife, Vera Ivanovna, lived at this time in the town of Berdyansk in the Ukraine. Pavel Datsko was free for less than a year. He was arrested in Berdyansk in March, 1939, and sentenced to ten years in labor camp without right of correspondence. He died in a camp in Siberia in 1941. His wife died a lonely old woman in Moscow in 1967.

In 1938, after his exile and not long before his arrest, Pavel Datsko said: "I want to write the history of Evangelical Christians Baptists in Russia from its very beginning." However, he was not destined to write the history of our brotherhood. But his literary legacy, his name, and his whole life have passed irrevocably into the history of our brotherhood as one of the true and courageous servants of the Gospel, a talented poet, and a martyr for God's cause.

"They shall be mine, says the Lord of hosts, my special possession on the day when I act . . . . Then once more you shall distinguish . . . between one who serves God and one who does not serve him" (Mal. 3: 17, 18).

Our evangelical brotherhood sings Datsko's hymns, and amid severe trials is making its way toward that heavenly country of which he wrote so movingly:

O my beautiful homeland,
The goal to which I yearn!
Each hour my song
Rings out to you from here.
A stranger here—my home is there;
For there is no chain
That can fetter my free spirit
Outside my homeland.

In my native land on earth
My life is a burning flame,
I cannot number here
The friends that God has given.
Yet still I strive toward Heaven
Through the burning heat of the journey;
I am there in spirit,
I yearn to enter there.

Although my path is narrow
And the thorny way is grim,
Strength is abundant
Amid the mountain of holy gifts.
My staff is God's Word;
His spirit is my treasure;
Only there in the land of consolation
Will I lay down my head to rest.

O, who will go there with me
To that beautiful Canaan?
There is perfect rest from toil,
Long ago I was called there.
Let us all go, all who suffer here,
For whom this world is strange,
Only there will you all find rest,
In the land that is my home!

JESUS CHRIST,
THE CENTER OF ALL EXISTENCE[6]

Our Lord Jesus Christ, at Caesarea Philippi, asked
His disciples this question about Himself: "Who do
men say that the Son of Man is?" Since that time 19
centuries have passed; and those who best represent
mankind have not arrived at a single definite answer.
Even today one hears the most contradictory opin-
ions; even today the personality of Christ is an enigma to many.

One cannot but admit that the personality of

[6]Paper written by Pavel Datsko, read at a group session of
Evangelical Christians-Baptists in Leningrad in 1926.

Christ is so many-sided and so unusual in our world that no human attempts to expose it and to present it in all its fullness can achieve their aim, for He is infinitely perfect. However, we cannot say that He is unknowable. It is precisely this that draws us to Him. We can recognize and feel that we know Him, but we can never put any limits to our knowledge of Him. As our knowledge of Him grows, new aspects of His many-sided personality are continually revealed to us, and every time such a revelation occurs it gives us, the faithful, inexpressible spiritual delight; it broadens our spiritual horizons and enriches our view of the world.

By His incarnation, by His life on earth and His dealings with publicans and sinners—says Professor Lyutard—Christ so abased Himself that we human beings are, so to speak, unable to realize that He is worthy to occupy a more honorable place in our ideas about Him. But no matter how exalted our ideas of Him are, His real position will surpass them all.

No single object of belief or worship among men has possessed or now possesses the wealth of glorious names that the Bible ascribes to Christ. Rapt in contemplation of His Lord, the Apostle to the Gentiles bears witness of Him as if he were hastening to climb a wonderful ladder of glorious names, the top of which rises to the heavens: "Therefore God has highly exalted him and bestowed on him the name which is above every name, that at the name of Jesus every knee should bow, in heaven and on earth and under the earth" (Phil. 2: 9, 10).

Thus, however exalted our knowledge of Christ, He always remains unsurpassed; and so our theme, in which I wish to magnify my Teacher and Lord, will not be too exalted for Him. And if the great and inspired Apostle to the Gentiles gives testimony of Him, that all things were created by Him and for Him, then I may boldly and gladly affirm that He is indeed the center of everything created by Him, the center of existence. And so our theme is: *Jesus Christ—the Center of All Existence.*

Everyone who hears this theme, even for the first time, will feel the greatness of the subject with which he is making contact. As I begin to develop so great a theme, I have no intention at all of producing something that will surpass all that has previously been written about Christ: I merely wish to give a particular direction to ideas that are already well known in Christian literature, so as to illuminate the given theme in a proper manner and to magnify the name of our Lord. For this reason I consider it necessary to approach the analysis of this most important subject as it concerns three different spheres of our existence: moral, historical, and cosmological.

When we turn to the person of our blessed Lord, and try to form an idea of His moral nature, the first and most important thing that fixes our attention on Him is the complete spiritual harmony of His inner world. This is precisely what we are unable to find in any other man. His moral nature is so great that we can say: He is more than moral, He is more than devout, and this means that He is holy in the full and proper sense of the word. If we simply examine the spiritual qualities whose divine beauty was expressed in His character with extraordinary clarity, we find there immaculate purity, peace, and bliss of soul.

This spiritual harmony of His inner world raised Christ above the level of all that has been achieved by mankind in this respect. The basic motive for all His movements and actions, and for the deeds He performed, was His unchanging love of the Father, and the reason for them was the temporal and eternal happiness of men. At the root of His character we can find nothing but close and uninterrupted contact with His Heavenly Father, from whom all His actions proceeded, and to whom He took everything.

No one has been able to find a single instance in the life of Christ at which His thoughts strayed from His Father. Even at the moment of inexpressible suffering on Golgotha, when He exclaimed: "My God, my God, why hast Thou forsaken me?" the union with the Father was not fundamentally broken, for He soon afterward cried out in triumph: "It is finished!" This moral union of Christ with God the Father at every moment of His life was so firm, so unshakable and complete, that He truly realized in His own person the idea of religion, whose purpose is precisely this—complete union with God. Thus He is the personal representative and the living incarnation of an ideal Christianity, of a true and absolute religion. If it can be said in general terms that love has appeared on earth at any time, then it was specifically in the person of Jesus Christ that it appeared, in this perfect image of gentleness and humility. But in this humble and gentle image of the Son of Man it is impossible not to see the light of a greatness that is not of this world, which prompts us involuntarily to bow down before Him. Who can look on Him as He goes quietly to and fro, without sensing a hidden greatness, without being aware that it shines through in all His deeds, and especially in His deep humility?

We may derive some measure of interest and inner contentment from fixing our attention on a second, no less important feature in the character of Christ: this is His universality in the sphere of morality and religion. When other men, even the best of them, contribute to the development of the idea of good and of perfection, they do so only to a very small degree. But Christ brings to perfection all that can be called great and virtuous. His inner world is a pure and beautiful paradise, full of flowers that shine under the azure vault of Heaven, flowers that send out their fragrance in the warmth of the sun's rays, and fill the contemplative spirit with bliss and joy.

The personality of Christ is a miracle. His combination of humility and majesty gives Him a unique aspect of divine holiness, and this produces in every unprejudiced man not only a feeling of amazement, but also a feeling of holy reverence and of worship. In Him we are aware of a fullness of perfection which infinitely exceeds the measure of the highest natural human development. This limitless fullness of perfection shown forth in the life and deeds of the Savior is so great and so all-embracing that learned scholars are unable after many years of the most serious and careful study to analyze even one aspect in sufficient detail and depth. It is quite appropriate at this point to recall the words of His beloved disciple, who said: "Many other things Jesus did; were every one of them to be written, I suppose that the world itself could not contain the books that would be written" (John 21: 25).

Not only individuals, but even whole societies are unable to develop to their full extent even one aspect of His character. He remains an inexhaustible source of example, and object for the highest aspirations of the human spirit. Medieval knights saw in Him the lofty ideal of knightly nobility; monks saw Him as the pattern of the purest and highest form of asceticism; philosophers saw in Him a man who knew the truth; for historians He explained the meaning of history; for metaphysicians He was the truest symbol of heavenly wisdom, the incarnation of an ideal moral perfection and the union of an ideal moral perfection and the union of the divine with the human. All these features may really be seen in the character of our Savior. He is noble, self-restrained, wise, ideally perfect, holy and pure; and He unites all these divine qualities with human ones. In this marvelous and perfect image an unprincipled man will discover the wonderful truth of the Gospel: "He was manifested in the flesh, vindicated in the Spirit, seen by angels, preached among the nations, believed on in the world, taken up in glory" (I Tim. 3: 16).

Humanity knows no more perfect pattern. And wherever a man may be, or to whatever degree he has developed, if his thoughts turn to virtue, they cannot rise higher than the pattern of the thoughts of our Savior; and if he began to look for a particular person in the history of mankind, there, amid the great and the powerful who have won a crown, his searching gaze would light upon none other than Christ crucified, wearing a crown of thorns, suffering, and in His sufferings forgiving. He, and only He, is to be a pattern for universal imitation in all respects. And therefore only He can turn to all men with the challenge that they should hate worldly vanity and follow Him.

The words with which Luke the Evangelist begins his account of the birth of Jesus Christ are very modest and very significant: "A decree went out from Caesar Augustus that all the world should be enrolled." Christ was born at this time. This census served as an occasion for the fulfillment of ancient prophecies that Jesus Christ would be born in Bethlehem, the ancient home of the house of David. The account, which is very simple in form, shows how the entry of Jesus Christ into history coincides with the highest point of fulfillment of ancient times. This fulfillment in the development of the history of the ancient world found its expression in the power of the emperor. The actual course of history in ancient times assisted the progress of sacred history to a considerable degree, and thus became one with it.

This idea of creating a single government and uniting many peoples under the supreme and limitless power of an emperor was the prevailing idea of the time. One could say that almost every Roman general entering the Capitol in a triumphal procession was a prototype of the emperor, who would no longer hand over his power to someone else, but would retain it forever. And already individual wielders of power who were arising out of the stormy movements of their time toward the end of the republic—such men as Pompey, Antony, Julius Caesar—were precisely the heralds and the forerunners of Him who was to estabish His power in the future and make it a lasting possession of His house. It was in this that the Roman world power reached

190

its highest point and the final fulfillment of its mission.

An early consciousness of the unity of all peoples on the one hand, and a passion for sovereign rule on the other, were the sources from which arose the idea of a union of all nations under one worldwide monarchy. This proud idea was boldly expressed by energetic wielders of power in the ancient world, such as Nebuchadnezzar, Cyrus, Alexander the Great, and Caesar Augustus. But we know that their attempts were not destined to succeed in that form or to the degree they desired. At the same time, in Israel, an ancient prophecy was set forth in the book of Daniel concerning the gradual replacement of various monarchies, whose highest point of development would coincide with the coming of the Kingdom of God and His saints.

Although the ancient world was unable to fulfill the idea of the unity of all nations, it nevertheless helped to propagate it and to strengthen it in men's minds, and by so doing made them ready for the great idea of the Kingdom of God. At the same time, the ancient world built roads by means of which the Gospel might reach all nations. The roads along which Roman officials and Roman legions traveled became roads along which the preachers of the Gospel made their missionary journeys. The whole world of that time was under the sway of one common power, created by mighty Rome. It was under the protection of this power that the young Christian church was to be born and to develop.

In the history of the ancient world, nations enter one after another onto the world stage; and as they come in turn, now rising, now falling, each of them shows a gradual decline in its historical importance in relation to its predecessor. They are like a range of hills whose height gradually diminishes, until they reach the plain of the turning point of world history.

In the book of the prophet Daniel the great kingdoms of the ancient world are represented in the form of the statue of a man: the head is of gold, the arms and breast of silver, the trunk and thighs of bronze—and the legs part iron and part clay. One cannot find a clearer and more accurate image to depict the gradual decline of the ancient world.

When the number of the gods had grown to an extraordinary extent, the egoism of sin reached its highest point and began to express itself in especially refined forms. At this point in the decline of morals, eternal love took the form of a man in order to heal the wounds of mankind, and to restore to the world unity, peace and love. Christ appeared after Plato had said that it would be necessary for some divine being to appear to prevent the human race from being swallowed up in a flood of depravity. Here was this very divine being. In the same manner, Plato expresses the universal expectation which is spoken of in the prophet: "And the desired of all peoples will come" (see also Haggai 2:7). He appeared at a time when all freedom had perished under the weight of despotism, all religious life had died under the influence of unbelief and superstition. He appeared like a light, illuminating every dark place.

Thus, Jesus Christ is the purpose of ancient history, the aspiration of universal development, the answer to the question with which ancient history ends, the solution to its enigma, the key to our understanding of world history. He is not a product of it, but a marvelous deed and miraculous gift of God. And as He is the aspiration and the expectation of history, so, although in His essence and in His origin He is not of the world, nevertheless in His situation on earth He united Himself with the history of our human life and became the purpose and the center to which the human spirit aspires, around which human thoughts turn; and the event around which human life shapes its course. With His appearance the old age ended, and a new age began.

As the pyramids tower above the plains of Egypt, so Christ in his spiritual greatness towers above all human leaders, teachers and founders of religion. And just as in the days when He was growing up on earth, so now He stands in the center of the great temple of the universe, and the eyes of all mortals are turned toward Him, the source and center of their being. He is at the center of world history. He stands, the great light of mankind, and illuminates the circle of human life with everlasting light. He calls to Himself the tired travelers of the world, and calms their troubled spirits with tranquil peace.

In the preceding sections of this paper, we have enough facts to convince us that our Lord Jesus Christ really is the center of our existence, both of the inner experiences which constitute our world, and of the phenomena and the events which constitute the history of mankind. However, if we stopped at this point, we should not be able to say that Jesus Christ is the center of our existence, for in the preceding sections we have dealt only with human existence without reference to the universe.

The idea was long held by mankind that the earth

on which we live is in fact the center of the universe. But as men's knowledge of the natural sciences increased, so did their knowledge of the universe, and men's thoughts began to seek another center which would be more in accordance with their wider ideas of the universe. After the invention of the telescope, the heavenly bodies were arranged in groups according to their size, and the distances between these bodies were calculated. The attention of scientists turned to the sun, as the largest heavenly body producing its own light, and exerting a controlling influence over the other planets adjacent to it. Then they discovered the physical laws in force which showed that all the heavenly bodies which come within the range of our observation are dependent on one another. Thus our world was proven to be one of the worlds that make up the solar system, and the sun was proclaimed as the center of this system. However, further study showed that our solar system is not the only one in the universe: astronomers say that there is an incalculable number of such systems, and that space itself is infinite.

Further scientific investigation showed that this infinite number of heavenly bodies is a complex of independent worlds, similar to our sun, moon, and so forth. All these worlds are controlled by strictly defined laws, and remain in a state of constant movement. This movement takes place, not in straight lines, but in infinite curved lines, forming innumerable ellipses which move ceaselessly in infinite space. For centuries, for millenia, we know not how long, this countless multitude of worlds has moved around in a majestic dance.

If we could conceivably occupy some neutral

place from which it would be possible to observe the universe, this magnificent spectacle would in truth be sufficient to last us all our lives. The countless number of worlds, the ceaseless movement, the infinity of space and time turn our thoughts toward eternity. The grandeur of creation speaks to us of a great, eternal power, and the rule of law throughout the universe bears witness to a mighty intellect, beyond our understanding, from whom all proceeded, by whom all is preserved, and for whom all things exist. It would be futile to look for some unmoving material center of a boundless and infinite universe, going out toward a shoreless ocean of eternity, a center around which these worlds move in procession. It would be futile to invent a name for such a center, for no name known to men comprises the sum of qualities which would be necessary for it to be applied to the center of existence of the universe. But without a center which would regulate the equilibrium of these worlds, the existence of a universe is unthinkable. There must be such a center. Our consciousness demands it, our reason demands it, the laws of the universe demand it. Such a center truly exists: its name is the Word of God, which is Christ. He is the center of all existence!

This understanding of the position of our blessed Lord in the universe is fully borne out by His immortal testimony concerning Himself: "From the beginning, I am!" This idea of Him is corroborated by the writers of the Bible, in both the Old and the New Testaments. The wisest of the Biblical writers speaks of Christ in a deeply prophetic spirit and in magnificent artistic images, when He describes Him as the Artist who sits at the center of the universe and sketches the outlines of the majestic picture of creation (Prov. 8). The Apostle to the Gentiles speaks of his Lord in no less magnificent words when he says: "He is the image of the invisible God, the first-born of all creation; for in him all things were created, in heaven and on earth, visible and invisible, whether thrones or dominions or principalities or authorities—all things were created through him and for him. He is before all things, and in him all things hold together" Col. 1: 15-17).

How much is expressed in these words! Our consciousness cannot comprehend the magnificence of creation. It surpasses our understanding. We do not have the words, nor the understanding, or the numbers to express it as it is in reality, and when we speak of the universe, we are compelled to use such expressions as infinite, unbounded, countless, and so on. However, all this greatness has a source and a center of its existence. "In him all things hold together"—and not only this—not only do all things hold together and maintain their existence through Him: He penetrates all that exists. We in our weakness are forced to resort to a vague understanding of infinity; but for Him there are definite numbers. And so we read: "He reckons the number of the stars; he calls each one of them by name."

THE UNFADING IDEAL OF CHRISTIANITY[7]

"I am continually with thee; thou dost hold my right hand. Thou dost guide me with thy

[7]Sermon preached by P. Y. Datsko on April 2, 1928, at a meeting in Moscow of Evangelical Christians-Baptists.

counsel, and afterward thou wilt receive me to glory. Whom have I in heaven but thee? And there is nothing upon earth that I desire besides thee. My flesh and my heart may fail, but God is the strength of my heart and my portion for ever. For lo, those who are far from thee shall perish; thou dost put an end to those who are false to thee. But for me it is good to be near God; I have made the Lord God my refuge, that I may tell of all thy works" (Ps. 73: 23-28).

In human life, my dear brothers and sisters, you may often hear it said that people choose ideals for themselves. Their ideals are of various kinds—personal, family, social, national; sometimes they are concerned with humanity in general. The aims set by these ideals carry mankind forward, and mankind strives to attain them. To be always striving—such is the permanent condition of the world; but it must be said that these aims are not always realized. It often happens that men expend great efforts and use up many resources, and devote most of their lives to the achievement of their aims; but these aims, like a mirage, like something unreal, disappear at the very moment when they seem to be within reach.

This often causes sorrow and disappointment. Those who do not attain their aims are inclined to give up life's struggle: life does not satisfy their spiritual needs. They remain empty, and this emptiness consumes their human hearts with anguish. How many of these broken hopes and expectations there are, my dear brothers and sisters.

But if one may speak of human ideals, of the ideals of men who do not know the truth, who are not illumined by the light of Christ, there is all the more reason why one may speak—and should speak—of the true ideals of the Christian life, of the ideals of believers. What I should like is this: that we should turn our thoughts in this direction at this time, that we should form a clear notion of our ideal, and that it should become the aim of our whole life, possess our whole being, and carry us forward. And so, dear brothers and sisters, I propose to you that we should meditate and talk for awhile concerning *the unfading ideal of Christianity.*

Of what does it consist, this ideal of Christianity, illumined by the light of Christ's teaching that never grows dim?

It does not, of course, consist in earthly achievements, or the earthly things that surround us. Nor does it consist in things that build up a man's pride and self-regard. Our Lord Jesus Christ says: "Woe to you, when men say of you, 'Well done.'" It is not our aspiration that men should say of us "Well done." This is not our ideal. Likewise, our Christian ideal does not lie in enrichment through knowledge. That is the world's idea; mankind expends much energy and many resources in pursuing it. The Lord tells us through the prophet Jeremiah that we should not be proud of knowledge, even if we possess it. And Paul says that if a man has all knowledge and has not love, he is nothing. Thus, the possession of great knowledge likewise does not constitute the ideal of Christianity.

Similarly, the ideal of our Christian life does not lie in the influence which we are able to exert upon the people about us. You know that when Christ sent His apostles to preach the Gospel of the Kingdom of

God, and when they returned with the joyful news "Lord, even devils are subject to us in thy name," Christ reproached them for their zeal and said, "Do not rejoice that devils are subject to you, but rejoice that your names are inscribed in heaven in the book of life." It is this to which our thoughts and our spiritual gaze should be directed. The psalm which we have read leads us into the inner world of the man of faith, in whom the ideal of life is disclosed. In it we read: "But I am always with thee . . ."

To abide always in personal contact with the Lord! That is the ideal of the man of faith. It is to this that our spirit must strive, this must be the constant aim of the man of faith. "I am always with thee."

The highest spiritual condition exists when we are able to establish this full and profound contact and union between ourselves and our Lord, and are able to say with David: "I am always with thee." At every moment of my life, in all circumstances, in difficulties, in grief, in trials, at every moment of my journey in thy footsteps, in all my actions and deeds, "I am always with thee." This spiritual state is the ground of our joy, the ground of our consolation and inexpressible happiness. How blessed is a man when he is able to feel and experience this, and to say, in the confidence of his hope in the Lord, "Yes, Lord, through thy mercy, through thy great love for me, through the gift of thy grace, I am what I am—I am able to be thy child, to be united with thee, and to live thy life."

This is one of the steps in our spiritual life as Christians. This can be the ideal to which our spirits can aspire. It can make our inner life rich and beautiful.

The psalmist further says: "God is my stronghold and my portion for ever."

You can see in this text how the psalmist takes a step forward in the spiritual life. He feels himself to be close by the Lord. He says, "Thou art always at my right hand." He feels this closeness and experiences His presence. And then he draws attention to something different. He says that the Lord has become his portion for ever. This means that the Lord has become his inheritance and his inalienable possession, so that nothing can separate him from the Lord; nor can the Lord abandon him, for He is his portion forever. How wonderful is this condition—this holy confidence in such nearness, such close contact with the Lord. This is our ideal. This is a further step in our spiritual life, when we are not only aware of the closeness of God, of the fact that He is with us, but when we also know that He is in us, that He will never abandon us. And this leads us to the next step in our spiritual life.

The Lord is the psalmist's stronghold—a stronghold that is hidden within him. How often we feel ourselves unstable and weak in the presence of influences that operate within us, or from without. How often we are powerless to resist hostile forces of one kind or another. How often we become aware of negative states of mind—feelings, perhaps or thoughts, or something else that desires to enslave us, and we are often ready to exclaim "wretched man that I am, who shall deliver me from this body of death?" And this means that the wonderful victory of the Lord has not yet been accomplished in us, that the Lord has not yet fully possessed our human hearts. The psalmist also means something else. All that disturbs and torments us is in the past; it is all forgotten. Another life is put before us, a life united with the Lord, and He is our stronghold.

The spirit of a man of faith, his heart, his will and intellect, his whole being, all are at peace and entirely safe in this stronghold. No passion, no temptation, no power in this world can shift this stronghold or make it totter. Thus does the Lord strengthen every individual soul, thus does He establish His Church. He has built His Church on this rock, on this stronghold, so that the gates of hell shall not prevail against it.

You see, again, that the psalmist moves still further forward; he comes to the point where he is completely liberated from all that is earthly. He says: "Whom have I in heaven? And when I am with thee, there is nothing upon earth that I desire."

Such is the condition which the man of faith can attain! His thoughts are in Heaven, his desires are in Heaven, his aspirations are directed to Heaven— to Him who is his portion, to Him who is the stronghold of his heart. This is that full possession of the Lord which constitutes the unalterable ground of his happiness in all the circumstances of his life, which constitutes such fullness of life that he says: "When I am with thee, there is nothing on earth that I desire," or he repeats the words of the apostle, "For me to live is Christ, to die is gain." In this condition, our life on earth is not attached to anyone or to anything. For the man of faith, this world becomes mere dross: the Christian is rewarded by the great gain, which is Christ. This wonderful, unfading ideal of Christianity finds its expression, as you see, not in earthly objects or forms, but in God alone, in possessing Him to such an extent that a man is liberated from the influences of his environment and cannot help expressing his attitude to it as one of renunciation: "There is nothing on earth that I desire."

If by the gift of God's grace we attain this condition, if the Lord thus possesses our heart, our intellect, and our will, He has really placed His throne in us and fulfilled His promise: "I will enter, I will take up my abode in them and I will be their God." And when this comes about, can there be any forces, any influences which can work on us? Of course not! A man who has reached this spiritual height is given the full armor of God, and sings a song of triumph:

Our sword is not of shining steel,
Not forged by man's hammer,
It was given to us by God Himself
As the flame of burning faith.
It severs the chain of sin
And gives freedom to the prisoner,
It paves the way through the wilderness
And leads that way to the Truth.

This is what the Lord provides for men of faith, this is how He gives to His own people the arms which are ever victorious. But these arms are not material, they are not the arms of the flesh, but of the spirit, which are able to destroy the strongholds of the devil. The psalmist says: "One thing God has said, twice I have heard, that power belongs to God." This too is true. Dear brothers and sisters, if we are zealous for the affairs of God, for our work in His harvest field, and for the fullness of spiritual life, it is in this truth that we find them all.

Everything exists in the Lord, in Him and only in Him. He is the rock from which flows the source of life; and so all our life is in our Lord, and only in Him.

How is this ideal attained?

The psalmist confesses that he is powerless and weak. He says: "My flesh and my heart waste away." This does not mean that he is speaking here of men who are physically strong, whose hearts are steadfast to an unknown degree. No! When the psalmist turns his gaze to his spiritual condition, he finds himself powerless and weak. He says: "My flesh wastes away." And it is true that by ourselves we are powerless; but he goes on to say: "He upholds me." The Lord holds me by the right hand. Like a small child, I am weak and cannot rise to this height: but you take me by my right hand.

This is what the Lord does! The Lord, changeless and strong, takes us by the right hand—weak and helpless as we are—and leads us. This where our strength lies; this is why we are able to rise to this spiritual height, and take up this wonderful position near our Lord.

In life, amid trials, amid temptations and many sorrows, we likewise have the wonderful assistance of our Lord. We read: "Thou leadest me by thy counsel." Our route goes through the valley of the shadow of death, and in it all kinds of dangers may arise. But the Lord accompanies us, He is always with us, He holds us by the right hand and He guides us by His counsel. This is the pledge of our success and of our triumph. Thus our experience makes us truly confident that the Lord will not leave us without His guidance and His counsel, that at difficult moments in life He will be there with His all-wise counsel, and will bring about whatever it is that we need. In this way He shows to us His loving kindness.

When is this ideal finally realized?

Since this ideal does not originate here on earth, it is not finally realized on earth. However, we can make the ideal our own, and we can attain to a condition in which we can experience the fullness of spiritual bliss and express our overflowing feelings in a song of joy. At the same time, we must admit that our ideal is not fully realized here. The psalmist says: "And afterwards thou wilt receive me into glory." It is to this far point that the rays of this wonderful light are directed! This ideal is realized in eternity.

This is in full accord with the views of the apostle, who says: "If for this life only we have hoped in Christ, we are of all men most to be pitied." Our ideal leads us further, and our journey ends in eternity. It takes us into glory. He enables us to see His glory.

Here is the end to which our gaze is turned—to the heavens to the lofty heights of Jerusalem. But this is not only something that we desire, something to which our spirit aspires. It is what our Lord has told us clearly. Our Lord Jesus Christ says, "In my Father's house there are many mansions." Yes, there are many mansions there. And in the 17th chapter of John we find Christ praying: "Father, I desire that they may be with me where I am, to behold my glory which thou hast given me before the foundation of the world."

How wonderful are the thoughts of God! John says, "Beloved, we are already the children of God." We have already attained this wonderful condition, "but it has not yet been revealed, what we shall be," it has not yet been revealed what we shall be when we have finished our earthly journey, for "we shall see him as he is." Then we shall see the end of all that is earthly and imperfect.

This will be the fulfillment of our wonderful, never-fading ideal, to which every man of faith aspires, which he desires and awaits. All else is but sand, dust, and ashes.

And so, dear brothers and sisters, I invite you, in the words of Paul,[8] "Let us lay aside every weight, and sin which clings so closely, and let us run with perseverance the race that is set before us," gazing upon Jesus Christ who accomplished this earthly journey, who entered into the eternal Holy of Holies, who dwells in the heavens and intercedes for us. To Him be glory for ever! Amen.

---

[8]Pavel Datsko evidently accepts the Pauline authorship of the Epistle to the Hebrews. Western scholars believe that Paul did not write this epistle. Acceptance of its Pauline authorship among Soviet Christians is an indication of the lack of theological education available in the Soviet Union.

9

Pavel Ivanov-Klyshnikov

1886-1941

ON JUNE 25, 1928, at the Fourth World Baptist Congress in Toronto, Canada, Pavel Vasilievich Ivanov-Klyshnikov, the Secretary of the Federal Baptist Union, delivered an address entitled "The work and tasks of Baptists in the USSR."

" . . . Among all the so-called sectarian currents in Russia, the Baptists were the most significant current as regards the number of followers, the strictest in defense of the purity of their doctrine, the most steadfast in the terrible persecutions of the Tsarist epoch, and the most strikingly ardent as regards the missionary spirit that burned within them!

We have no precise statistics. We have approximately 200 thousand baptized members.

It is clear from this that evangelization has barely touched the Russian people. In many places people have never heard the preaching of the Gospel.

For 4,000 communities and groups we have about 900 pastors, and 3,100 communities and groups are left without trained leaders. For 5,000 local churches we own only about 400 prayer houses, and we have about 800 rented ones, but the other 3,800 churches are in private homes.

Our work in the USSR is still in this embryonic state. Nevertheless, the Russian people are exceptional in the depth of their religious feelings and its religious quest. Theirs is the most fruitful spiritual soil among all the peoples of the earth. They are a God-seeking people, a God-bearing people, in the words of Russian philosopher Vladimir Solovyov.

Side by side with this task of evangelization we are faced by no less a task within our communities: educational work . . .

What I wanted to emphasize especially . . . was this, that the evangelization of our land has a world-wide significance in the development of God's work on earth.

Russia is not Europe, but she is not Asia either: she is a mediator between two worlds. And the light of Christ which will flare up in her will light and warm both the West and the East" (*The Baptist*, 1928, No. 7, pp. 4, 5).

The 7,000 participants of the World Congress listened with great attention to Pavel Ivanov-Klyshnikov's speech, since he was speaking in the name of the Russian brotherhood, which had preserved its faithfulness to God at the time of the most cruel persecutions under the Tsarist regime, and had raised high the banner of evangelization after 1917. Pavel Ivanov-Klyshnikov himself came from a long line of Russian Protestants.

It will not be without interest to acquaint the reader with certain facts from the life and work of his father, one of the pioneers of the Russian Evangelical-Baptist movement, Vasily Vasilievich Ivanov-Klyshnikov.

Vasily Ivanov-Klyshnikov came from a *Molokan*[9] family. From his early years he was distinguished by a zealous quest for God's truth. In 1870 he got to know the small ECB church in Tiflis, which numbered ten members at that time, and decided to receive baptism by immersion according to the Word of God. However, when he was interviewed, the believers of the church refused him baptism, pointing to the necessity for belief in the forgiveness of sins and to a personal spiritual communion with God.

Vasily Ivanov-Klyshnikov began to study God's Word sincerely with profound meditation and prayer.

A year later, in 1871, the Tiflis church again put him seriously to the test. Convinced of his regeneration, they admitted him to baptism by immersion. The baptism was performed by N.I. Voronin. From that day Vasily Ivanov-Klyshnikov began to labor in God's harvest field. Thanks to his prayers and his witness for Christ in the village of Novo-Ivanovka (in the Transcaucasus) there was formed the second (at that time) Evangelical Christian-Baptist Church in our land after the Tiflis one.

Vasily Ivanov-Klyshnikov visited hundreds of towns and villages, preaching Christ crucified. For

[9]The *Molokans* of "milk-drinkers" were a Russian sect who rejected the Orthodox emphasis on ritual and claimed the right to live according to the Scripture.

his zealous evangelistic labors he was subjected to persecution from the authorities of that time.

For about ten years Ivanov-Klyshnikov was forced into an illegal position while he continued to perform his work in God's harvest field. From 1890 he contributed to the Evangelical Christian-Baptist journal *Discussion*, which was published secretly. He took a fervent part in many congresses of our brotherhood, beginning with the first in 1879 in Tiflis.

In 1895 Vasily Ivanov-Klyshnikov was arrested in Baku as a very dangerous criminal, and sent off into exile in the town of Slutsk for five years. He passed in shackles along many kilometers of the prisoners' road, through prisons in Tiflis, Novorossiissk, Feodosiya, Kiev, Kovelya, Warsaw . . .

After serving his term of exile, he worked for long years among the believers of the Transcaucasus.

On February 10, 1919, Vasily Ivanov-Klyshnikov passed away. He said to his son Pavel: "I am going home!"

Pavel Ivanov-Klyshnikov turned out to be a worthy successor in the preaching of the Gospel to the Russian people. Well educated and talented, and with a fervent love for the Lord, he contributed with much blessing to our Christian press, and especially to the journal *The Baptist*, where dozens of his articles were published. Among them is an outstanding article about Valtasar Gubmaier, a courageous and faithful preacher of the Gospel in the 16th century, who was burnt at the stake in 1528 in Vienna (*The Baptist*, No. 3, 1928).

In his articles, Ivanov-Klyshnikov called our evangelical brotherhood to follow courageously after

Christ and to witness widely to Him, and not only among the Slavonic people . . . In January 1926, in the article "Tasks of Baptists in the USSR for 1926" (*The Baptist*, No. 1-2, 1926), he wrote:

> As always, most attention will be paid to the preaching of the Gospel. In 1926 the work of evangelization will go in the same direction as in 1925, embracing more and more new places. More attention than formerly will be paid to preaching among Christians of other nations— Armenians, Georgians, Ossetians, and others. In 1926 we intend to promote with particular force the slogan: "Christ for the pagans and Muslims living in the USSR." There are about three million pagans and half-pagans in our land: Kalmyks, Buryats, Chuvash, Cheremisy, Mordvinians, Zyryans, Votyaks, Permyaks, Chukchi, Eskimos, and others. They are scattered in the Volga regions and in Siberia. There are about fourteen million Muslims in the USSR: Tatars, Kirgizians, Bashkirs, Nogaitsy, Lezghins, and others. The foundations of missionary work among both the pagans and the Muslims have already been laid down for us. But still it all lies before us. The image of the Macedonian stands persistently before us with the words: "Come and help us."

Now, in the 1970's, hundreds of believers in Komi (Zyryans), the Chuvash, the Mordvinians, the Mariitsy, Udmurts, and other small peoples in our land pray to Christ in their native languages. This is God's answer to the prayers and the labor of the

211

Russian Evangelical Christian-Baptist brotherhood.

In 1926, the 26th congress of Christians Baptists took place in Moscow, and Pavel Ivanov-Klyshnikov was elected Secretary of the Federal Union of Baptists. The next three years were the most blessed and fruitful of his life and work.

In 1925 he took an active part in the organization of preachers' Bible courses. (They were opened with God's help in 1927 in Moscow.)

In May, 1928, he participated in the work of the Fifth All-Ukrainian Congress of Baptists in Kharkov, where he delivered a report on the Bible courses. The Congress of Ukrainian Baptists was filled with deep gratitude to the Lord for the work of the courses and expressed their thankfulness to all the lecturers through Ivanov-Klyshnikov.

In June, 1928, he took part in the Fourth World Baptist Congress where he was elected to the Executive Committee of the World Baptist Congress.

But in 1929 a new period of persecution in our land was already imminent. Pavel Ivanov-Klyshnikov underwent three years' exile in Kazakhstan.

After he had finished his term of exile he was arrested again in October 1932 and sentenced to ten years in camp.

Until 1937 Ivanov-Klyshnikov's family had periodic meetings with him in the camp and kept up correspondence. But from 1937 the meetings and correspondence stopped abruptly. He never did return home to his family, but died in the camp in 1941. For many long years his family did not know whether he was alive or dead . . .

Along with Pavel Ivanov-Klyshnikov, his wife

Anna went through great trials. In 1941 she was arrested, as a Christian, and as the wife of a servant of the Gospel, and spent 11 years in prison. Six children were left without a father or mother. But the Lord did not abandon them. Two of them were sheltered during the war in the house of a believing sister, Alexandra Semirech, who lived in Omsk and did much good for the families of Christian prisoners.

Anna Ivanov-Klyshnikov returned from prison in 1952. Soon after her release she went to the Lord.

The Evangelical Christian-Baptist brotherhood holds Pavel Ivanov-Klyshnikov in remembrance. He remained faithful to the Lord to the end and died a martyr's death for the work of God in our land.

The Evangelical Christian-Baptist brotherhood does not know where Ivanov-Klyshnikov's grave is, nor does it know the date of his death. But the work of God to which he dedicated his life has not died or come to a halt. The Church of Christ lives and will continue to live and bear witness of salvation to a perishing world until the day of its rapture, for the Lord said: "I will build my church, and the powers of death shall not prevail against it" (Mt. 16: 18).

LETTER FROM PRISON

May 14, 1933

My dear beloved wife and darling children:
Irusenka, Alyosha, Kolya, Anya and Vasya,

I expect that tomorrow or the day after I will have a meeting with you. But you can't say everything during a prison meeting, so I am writing to you to supplement what I will tell you at our meeting.

During seven and a half months of separation I have longed for you with all my heart. For days on end, looking through the barred window to the scrap of blue sky and the peak of the mountain chain in the east, I think of you, and the hand of Almighty God keeps you and me.

The investigation has finished, and since I have committed no crime before the government, it is quite possible that I will be with you somewhere in a new place. May the Lord send us that joy!

But we disciples and fellow workers of the Lord Jesus Christ must be prepared for people who hate us without cause to treat us severely. Therefore we will also be ready for a long separation. I am full of joy now when I think that the time will come when we will be inseparable forever. That will be at the end of our earthly life, when we will meet again, after a temporary separation, in the Kingdom of our Lord.

Now, admitting the possibility of a long separation, I want to bless you each individually.

My dear wife Anna!

I bless you as the co-inheritor of abundant life, as my fellow laborer in the work of God and as the mother and teacher of our children. Together we carry the cross of Christ, and together we will rejoice before His face, but He will give us the happiness of work together in His harvest field for many years yet. And then, sated with length of days, He will take us to His dwelling-place, having let us see our children entering our blessed work!

Dear Irusenka!

I bless you, my beloved daughter! In the early morning of your life you have stood face to face with need and sorrow, and your child's shoulders are bent under the weight of the cross. But the Lord has given you the energy and courage of your mother and the endurance of your father. He has prepared happiness for you on earth and bliss in eternity. Therefore do not despair, but on the contrary rejoice!

My dear, beloved Alyosha!

I bless you as my eldest son. Your child's eyes have already gazed into the black abyss of suffering since armed men took your father from you. But God sees your tender heart and knows how you are able to love warmly and suffer deeply. He has prepared consolation for you in the love of God and men. You will find your happiness in work together with those near and dear to you.

My dear, good Kolya!

The Lord has endowed you with strength, and together with your brothers and sisters has appointed you to great service in Christ's work. I want to supplement God's blessings to you with my fatherly blessings. Be happy, my son, and always watch that you do not offend your brothers and sisters in any way. Treat Alyosha especially with full respect as the eldest brother and my deputy; always consult with him about everything.

My dear, darling Seryozha!

Through my prayers and those of your mother, the Lord has preserved your life, which has already been exposed several times to serious danger, and in 1927 He clearly showed me He would heal your illness. Your development is hampered due to the illnesses you have endured, but the Lord has appointed you to give glory to His name. He has endowed you richly. I give you my blessing to praise the Lord with that poetic and artistic gift, and to be

215

happy among those who are near and dear to you.

My dear little daughter Anya!

You are a living reminder of our banishment for the name of Jesus. You will be our consolation in old age. You pass calmly and safely through every storm and tempest, because God has given you the gifts of fearlessness and trust in Him. I wish you, my dear daughter, to pass through life happy and self-sacrificing in the name of God.

My darling, dear Vasya!

The sky above you will not be covered with clouds. With a clear brow you will offer up prayers to God, and they will always be heard.

Your birth almost entailed the death of your mother—remember that and love your mother especially. I give you my blessing to fulfill your service in life for the Kingdom after the example of your grandfather Vasily.

Children, love your mother very much and obey her instructions without any criticism because she bears great difficulties both for you and for me.

My darling wife! At our meeting I was infinitely consoled and encouraged by you: you were as bright and cheerful as the spring sun. I kiss you warmly.

Pavel

Dedicated to my wife,
Anna Petrovna Ivanova-Klyshnikova, nee Stryukova.

The fulfillment of my youthful fancies,
The embodiment of past dreams,
The blessing of the Almighty,
And my delight—is you!

You had no time to peer at life
With your pure heart and penetrating gaze
Before I came, both close to you and remote,
And together we set out on our journey.

For you and I, my dear, this path
Is a path of spiritual triumphs and victories,
And it leads us to a wonderful land
Where an unfading light shines.

Inspired by our common aspiration
You helped me in my labors,
A sensitive guardian of the
   purity of convictions,
Of the loftiness of sacred ideals.

It was a joy for me to be with you,
My faithful friend, my dear wife . . .
The prison door has closed behind me,
You are left alone with the children.

You languish in separation, my love,
You tremble like a sensitive doe;
That is a concession to a suffering heart,
An involuntary tribute to the nerves.

You have spent many dragging, cheerless days
And nights of sleeplessness,
You have shed many unconsoled, scalding tears
In the silence of the night.

You had to work painfully
To obtain daily bread for the children;
You have fought like a lioness for the children,
You have suffered like a mother for me.

Your cup of suffering is full,
The way of struggle is everlastingly long.
But the higher the wave of trials,
The fuller the torrent of grace.

The sun of eternal love in the
    glorious distance
Has continued to shine for you;
Every day on the tablets of your heart
You can write "Ebenezer"![10]

November 15, 1946
(Anna Petrovna's letter to Pavel Ivanov-
Klyshnikov—not sent).[11]

My dear, never-to-be-forgotten husband, Pavel.
Today, on your birthday,
I congratulate you in my thoughts with
    all my heart.
And from the bottom of my soul I wish you
    steadfast faith,
Hope, strength, endurance, and joy.
I would so much like to be with you on this day,
To embrace you, console and caress you,
    to tell you
All about those you love, and who is still alive:
    our children and I
Remember you all the time and send our loving
    and affectionate greeting.

[10]Stone of help.
[11]Anna Petrovna wrote this letter five years after her husband's death; obviously she had no idea that he had died.
(Translator's note.)

It is the fourteenth year since you were
    deprived of freedom,
The ninth that you have lived without
    right of correspondence.
What have you thought, what have you suffered
    in that time?
Almighty God knows that, and so do you.
Toward the end of the fifth year that I languished
    in captivity
I had to suffer painfully in prison.
Your sufferings now are so close, so familiar,
And how plain and clear to me it is what you have
    endured all these years.
You left me young, in the flower of youth
    and strength, and now I am different,
You left your six children as babies,
    and now they are not so,
And if you are foreordained by the Creator
    to return to us, you will not recognize us.

But I know that you love us
    more strongly than before
And when we meet you will embrace us
    with joyfulness and tender caresses.
All this time I have lived as your widow
And have kept totally faithful to you.
But time and distance have forced me
To grow accustomed to the idea that
    you are not with us.
Now I do not weep bitter tears over you,
And I do not grieve as I did before.
For many years now I have waited for you . . .
Whether or not I shall wait until the end,
    I do not know.

But I know that we shall meet beyond the grave,
Where there is no sadness, grief and separation,
   where joy, happiness and rest await us.

I know that I did not meet you on earth by chance,
But the Lord Himself united us with the
   bonds of love and marriage,
And appointed us a hard path
   according to our strength.
I am grateful to the Lord for our life together,
For all the sufferings, and for His love
   and mercy to us.
How many times in my life I have been
   near to death
But He protected me and kept me for this life,
So how can I be ungrateful or offended
   by the Creator?
Does not the Creator have power over the created,
Is it not happiness to be His creature?
It is now the fiftieth year of my life,
But I have never written poetry until now.
I rejoice and weep from excitement, like a child,
Because the good Muse has visited me now
   in bondage.
My dear Pavel,
Today in a bygone year your sixtieth year
   passed away.
How few bright days have you seen
   in the years you have lived?
First childhood—full of anxiety and worry,
Because of your father, who was hunted
   and persecuted by the police.
He was the first Baptist in Russia
And for that he endured exiles and prisons.

Then long study while in need,
    living on brass farthings, then
Strenuous work for a morsel of daily bread,
Worry about a large, needy family.
And life in recent years—continuous torment.
Now, my friend, I want to tell you
    about our dear children.
Your eldest daughter, Irina,
Is clever, good, and just.
From her very cradle until now she is
Quiet, modest, and obedient.
In her own family she has always
    behaved selflessly,
And although there were no conditions for study
    (she had to give up studying twice),
She finished medical institute
    one of the best students, with excellent marks.
Your three sons, Alyosha, Kolya, and Seryozha,
    are tall,
Fine boys, and all of them look like you.
And our two babies are growing up and studying.
A year ago they gave themselves to the Lord
    and were baptized,
Which illuminated my life
    with rays of joy and happiness.
I am happier than you, my friend,
    I know all about our children!
May the Lord bless you in your walk before Him,
And may He send to you on your journey
    the pillar of smoke and the pillar of fire,
So that you may reach the eternal Homeland,
    the radiant, holy Homeland,
And attain the glorious crown on your head
And be clothed in a white robe.

10

Alexandra Semirech

I HAVE HAPPY MEMORIES of our dear sister in the Lord, Alexandra Ivanovna Semirech.

A simple Russian woman with a strong face; stocky, with robust health and a gruff, almost masculine voice, she had a kind, sensitive heart, and a deep and sincere faith in God. She also possessed exceptional courage and the ability to encourage timid and weakened Christians in the years of persecution.

Alexandra Ivanovna was descended from native Siberians, hardened in the struggle with the grim forces of nature and the adversities of life. She lived almost all her life in Omsk. She became a believer when she was married and had three children. Her husband was a confirmed drunkard who did her much harm. But she did a great deal of good for her husband and her family, and for many believers.

Alexandra Ivanovna's house was a refuge for many persecuted and outcast people. With goodwill and zeal she continued in our days the ministry of Gaius, the host to strangers (Rom. 16: 23).

From 1937-38 the blind poetess Polina Yakovlevna Skakunova lived in her house. She had broken with atheism in the 1920's and had wandered around a good deal, and in 1938 she was arrested for confessing faith in Christ.

From 1941-44 the two children of the Christian prisoner Ivanov-Klyshnikov were in her house after the arrest of his wife, Anna Petrovna.

From 1943-44 Alexandra Ivanovna together with another sincere and virtuous Christian woman, Yevdokiya Samoilovna Varnavskaya, sought out believing prisoners in one of the camps situated on the outskirts of the town. These were members of a group of Christian young people arrested in the Crimea in 1940 for conducting a Christian young people's meeting and sentenced to five to ten years. In the difficult years of the war Alexandra Ivanovna and Yevdokiya Samoilovna apportioned food for parcels for these Christian prisoners from their own less than modest shares.

From 1943-44 Alexandra Ivanovna was one of the most active and fervent organizers of the renewal of regular meetings for divine worship in Omsk. A simple, uneducated woman, she was a fiery preacher of the Gospel at the Omsk meetings.

At the end of 1961, by which time she was extremely old, she traveled to Chelyabinsk to establish links with the Action Group of the Evangelical Christian-Baptist Church. Alexander Afanasevich Shalashov told me about this: he was the pastor of

Chelyabinsk church, and is now at rest with the Lord.

Shortly after this she went away peacefully to the Lord.

Peace be with you, dear laborer for the Lord!

11

Alexander Shalashov

1891-1963

"Remember your leaders, those who spoke to you the word of God; consider the outcome of their life, and imitate their faith" (Heb. 13: 7).

The year 1971 was the eightieth anniversary of the birth of Alexander Afanasevich Shalashov, an evangelist of the Volgo-Kamsky Evangelical Christian-Baptist Union from 1920 to 1928, a member of the Organizing Committee of Evangelical Christians Baptists during 1962-63, and pastor of the Chelyabinsk church. He passed into eternity on December 7, 1963.

Alexander Afanasevich did much blessed work in God's harvest field, and endured imprisonment and great trials for the name of Christ. For eighteen years he was ill and bedridden. Then he was healed by the Lord and sent to the work of the spiritual revival of the Evangelical-Baptist brotherhood.

Many believers remember Alexander Afanasevich with love—a kind, simple, sympathetic Christian; a faithful, courageous, tried and tested servant of God; a man of principle in questions of faith, who stood up dauntlessly in defense of the work of evangelism at a critical moment when there was a breach in the house of God.

Alexander Afanasevich was born on June 4, 1891, in the town of Minora in the Chelyabinsk region. In 1915 he came to believe in the Lord and subsequently underwent baptism by immersion in Khabarovsk Evangelical Christian-Baptist Church. Having joined Christ's Church, Alexander Afanasevich dedicated his whole life to preaching the Gospel.

In 1919 he was ordained by brother D. S. Olshansky in Samara (now Kuibyshev) to serve as an evangelist. During the ten years from 1919 to 1929 Alexander Afanasevich worked zealously in the Volgo-Kamsky Evangelical Christian-Baptist Union, preaching and organizing the churches of God in Povolzhe and the Urals.

At the same time Alexander Afanasevich took a very lively interest in the spiritual life of his own Far East brotherhood, where he had first become a believer.

The journal *Evangelist,* which was printed in Vladivostok, published a letter in 1921 from Alexander Afanasevich under the heading:

KIEV FARM
UFIMSKY DISTRICT.

We wish that the Lord may open up to you His good heavenly treasure house and from it give abundant gifts to all His children in the Far East.

Next, a warm greeting to all those who love the Lord and who know me personally. I became a believer and promised to serve my Lord in Khabarovsk in 1915.

Dear brother R. A.! Our esteemed and long-awaited journal, preaching peace, which you sent, has once more reached us living here in pagan Galilee, at the foot of the Urals. Tears of divine happiness shone in our eyes when we saw it, and we listened once more to its words with an attentive ear.

After a long and tiring wait, we have heard the words of many witnesses of the Gospel truth, and have again refreshed the thirsting soul (Prov. 25: 25). Once more the clearly printed words of the work of God's children have shone before us and we have gathered in the house around the good *Evangelist*. We have listened avidly to the news from a distant land (but our native land) of how the children of God are bearing the heat, affliction, and horrors of the day, and rejoice as at the gathering in of the vine.

O God, grant that this our joy may not cease forever, although "the fig tree do not blossom, nor fruit be on the vines, the produce of the olive fail and the fields yield no food, the flock be cut off from the fold and there be no herd in the stalls, yet I will rejoice in the Lord, I will joy in the God of my salvation" (Hab. 3: 17-19).

229

I remain your warmly affectionate friend, the least of the co-laborers in God's work.

A. Shalashov

(From the journal *Evangelist,*
No. 5, May 1921, p. 79.)

In 1929 the persecutions began. The Volgo-Kamsky Union was closed. During these years Alexander Afanasevich continued to preach the Gospel in communities in the towns of Artemovsk, Mozdok, and Makhachkaly. At the same time he worked as a blacksmith. In 1934, as a result of occupational injury, Alexander Afanasevich was paralyzed for many long years.

However, despite his serious illness which kept him entirely bedridden, he was arrested in 1936 as a servant of God and lay for five years in the prison hospital in Kharkov.

After his release from prison in 1941 Alexander Afanasevich remained bedridden until 1956. These were hard years both for himself and for his wife, Lukeria Filippovna. But even under these conditions Alexander Afanasevich wanted to be useful for the work of the Lord. His house in Mozdok, and later in Uman and Chelyabinsk, became a place for believers to visit. Many came to him for advice and encouragement. Many also prayed for the healing of this dear servant. The Lord heard His children's prayers, and so in 1956, after eighteen years of serious ailment, Alexander Afanasevich rose from his sickbed. The Lord healed him and once again entrusted him with a great service to the Church.

The believers of Chelyabinsk elected him their pastor, and he performed this ministry until the day of his death.

The Chelyabinsk church endured great trials. In 1958 their prayer house was taken away and the 300 believers of Chelyabinsk were forced to gather for divine worship in various private houses, but even these meetings were constantly subject to persecution.

When the Action Group of Evangelical Christians Baptists was formed in 1961, the Chelyabinsk church was one of the first to respond to God's summons to revival. Alexander Afanasevich, a faithful servant of God, grown wise with great spiritual experience, supported the work of the Action Group with his whole soul.

Even before the beginning of the work of the Action Group and the Organizing Committee, Alexander Afanasevich had carried on a great spiritual work among the unregistered churches of the Urals in regulating their services, in the election and ordination of pastors, and in the uniting of the Evangelical Christian-Baptist churches of the Urals among themselves. The believers of the Urals felt great love for Alexander Afanasevich.

In 1962 He was elected to the Organizing Committee of Evangelical Christians Baptists as the representative of the churches of the Urals. Despite his extreme old age, Alexander Afanasevich took a most active part in the work of the Organizing Committee. He visited a large number of the churches of the Urals, the central regions of Russia, the Ukraine, and Siberia. He ordained many young ministers in

231

1962-63 for the great work of spiritual revival in our brotherhood.

An old, experienced worker of the Volgo-Kamsky Evangelical Christian-Baptist Union, making use of his deserved authority among the brotherhood, Alexander Afanasevich, together with Sergei Terentevich Golev and Matvei Petrovich Kondrashov, was, as it were, the connecting link between the old generation of faithful servants of the Evangelical-Baptist brotherhood, who for the most part had laid down their lives in the camps, and the new generation, called by the Lord to service in the 1960's.

Alexander Afanasevich possessed great charm of soul. People's hearts clung to him; it was a joy to talk to him. He had an especially moving attitude of fatherly love to Gennadi Konstantinovich Kryuchkov, who performed his ministry in very complex and difficult circumstances, undergoing constant persecution. Every time they met again after trips around the churches, Alexander Afanasevich would embrace brother Kryuchkov with tears in his eyes and say joyfully: "You're alive! And safe! And free! Praise God!"

Alexander Afanasevich had a fine powerful bass voice. I remember that one day after one of our fraternal conferences in 1963 he sang his favorite hymn: "O, no, no one in the universe will deprive the faithful of their freedom!" It was good to watch this old man, gray with age, courageous, tempered in trials for the faith of Christ, and having been raised up once again in the breach in the house of God!

In 1962-63 Alexander Afanasevich put his signature to several very important documents of the Organizing Committee of Evangelical Christians

Baptists. In these years thousands of believers of registered and unregistered Evangelical Christian-Baptist churches were petitioning the government in writing for permission to convene an Evangelical Christian-Baptist congress under the leadership of the Organizing Committee.

In October 1963 the Council for the Affairs of Religious Cults, wishing to put an end to the campaign of petitions for a congress, and disregarding the will of the petitioners, permitted the All-Union Council to hold an all-union conference, subsequently renamed a congress.

The aim of the All-Union Council, however, was to lead the whole Evangelical Christian-Baptist brotherhood into error by the means of holding a fictitious congress (a pseudo-congress) and condemning the Organizing Committee's campaign for a congress. Four hundred men with the right to vote attended the conference. Delegates' passes for the congress were distributed to them, a congress agenda was produced, there were reports, accounts, speeches, elections, and so on—all this was meant to create the illusion of a genuine congress. The participants in the conference were accommodated in the Moscow hotel. "Turist" buses were allotted for their disposal, and so on. But at that time the true initiators of the congress were languishing in the prisons and camps of the land.

The Council for Religious Affairs and the All-Union Council had prepared well for their congress. This is how one of the prisoners wrote about it:

Som men slept peacefully in a hotel,
Other men dozed on plank beds:

233

Some abandoned Christ's commands,
    Others suffered for the faith.

The Organizing Committee sent its representatives to this conference, headed by Alexander Afanasevich.

Cold autumn rain was falling. About 50 believers stood in front of the All-Union Council building in Moscow. Among them was a tall old man in a raincoat, leaning on a stick—Alexander Afanasevich. He was not allowed into the building, and he stood in the rain outside for more than an hour.

After this he became seriously ill. At the end of October, 1963, a group of brothers and sisters saw Alexander Afanasevich off to his home. He left from Paveletsky station in Moscow. Everyone sensed that this was their last meeting, their parting with the dear old minister. The brothers and sisters wanted to see once more his good, brave face, to hear for the last time his fatherly parting words.

Suddenly, into the station waiting room came Gennadi Kryuchkov. He had also come to say farewell to his dear comrade in the ministry. Alexander Afanasevich became agitated and said: "Why have you come here? Why, they're looking for you everywhere. They could arrest you right here! Go away!"

When we had seated him in the carriage and we ourselves were crowding around the window, Alexander Afanasevich waved his hand to us for the last time, and on the glass of the window traced out several times: I Peter 5: 1-3. We could not receive his pastor's blessing and good wishes without tears. The train moved off, taking dear Alexander Afanasevich away from us ... One of the sisters from the Ukraine accompanied him as far as Chelyabinsk.

We went away sadly from the station ...

When he arrived home in Chelyabinsk, Alexander Afanasevich took to his bed for the last time. He asked that on the wall opposite his bed should be hung the small bag which held his Bible, and that his stick should be stood there. These were his invariable companions in his journeys throughout the country. He often looked at them, remembering his numerous visits to believers.

Alexander Afanasevich's friends and relatives felt that his heart was straining toward the church, to God's boundless harvest field where there was so much work to be done.

However, our old brother realized that his earthly path was coming to an end—that the Lord was recalling him into His everlasting dwelling-place. In these days many friends in the faith and in the ministry visited Alexander Afanasevich. He encouraged everyone and strengthened them spiritually, urging then to act courageously for the faith of the Gospel.

In the first days of December, 1963, Alexander Afanasevich received two notices from the KGB in Chelyabinsk—summonses for questioning. But he was so weak that he could not visit this institution which displayed so great an interest in believers.

On December 7, 1963, Alexander Afanasevich passed into eternity.

He left us all a good example of Christian longsuffering, gentleness, faithfulness to the Lord, selflessness and courage in the face of persecutions and trials. For very many believers he was a good father and leader. His pastor's parting words from the first epistle of Peter have always remained in the memory of the servants of the revived church:

"So I exhort the elders among you . . . Tend the flock of God that is your charge, not by constraint but willingly, not for shameful gain but eagerly, not as domineering over those in your charge but being examples to the flock" (5: 1-3).

12

Pavel Zakharov

1922-1971

May the grace and peace of God in the Holy
Spirit increase greatly in you, my dear and
beloved friends. I greet you with feelings of
deep love and a sincere heart, I, the least of you,
who was among you, but now am separated,
like many friends in Christ.

May His strength in you increase and may you
be able to bear all abuse for His work. The Lord
be with you always and in everything. John 15:
14-21.

Dear friends, remember me and all of us
prisoners in your prayers. We believe that the
Lord is our justification, and He will overcome
those who struggle with Him and will stand up
in defense of His suffering people. Give greet-

ings to all the brothers and sisters who labor and to all who love the Lord. May His will be done to the glory of His name.

Yours sincerely,
the least of all:
Pavel Zakharov

This is an extract from a letter of Pavel Frolovich Zakharov, a Christian prisoner, which was passed in 1964 to brothers serving on the Organizing Committee of Evangelical Christians Baptists from the Potma labor camp in Mordovia.

It was a good and long-awaited piece of news from our dear brother and co-laborer in God's harvest field, whose life and service were inseparably linked with the work of spiritual revival in the Evangelical-Baptist brotherhood. We were encouraged by our prisoner brother's cheerful spirit and by his hope in God's might. Over the last ten years Pavel Zakharov has twice been in prison. After each release he joined in the labor in God's harvest field.

But now our brother is not with us . . . On July 1, 1971, Pavel Zakharov's heart was stilled and he passed away. The hearts of his friends and relatives were wrung with grief: but he left an example of faithfulness to the Lord.

Our dear brother endured much suffering for the faith of Christ. On February 24, 1945, he was arrested as a Christian, for the first time, and was sentenced by a *troika* to five years' imprisonment. He served this term in "Ivdal" camp in the Urals.

In 1950, after the end of his five-year term, Zakharov was sent to the north of Krasnoyarsk district. In 1954 he returned from exile and settled in the town of Zhdanov in the Ukraine. Here also, however, he was subjected to a search of his house (in May 1955) and to threats.

In 1955 Zakharov moved to the town of Prokopievsk in Siberia. Here he took part zealously in the ministry of the local church as a preacher, a leader of music, and later an ordained evangelist.

In 1961, when the call to revival in our brotherhood was heard, Pavel Zakharov, along with the whole Evangelical Christian-Baptist church in Prokopievsk, responded to God's summons.

However, the enemies of God's work were not asleep. On October 20, 1962, the Rudichni Executive Committee of Prokopievsk passed a resolution demanding the exile of P.F. Zakharov for five years because of his preaching activity.

But the Lord preserved him from exile.

In 1962 he was elected by the believers of Siberia to serve on the Organizing Committee of Evangelical Christians Baptists. The period from 1962 to February 1964 was especially fruitful in Pavel Zakharov's ministry. During these years he visited hundreds of registered and unregistered communities in Siberia, Kazakhstan, Central Asia, the Urals, European Russia, the Ukraine, and the Baltic region.

Pavel Zakharov participated with fervor in the publication of the journal "Herald of Salvation." The very name of the journal was borrowed from a poem he had written.

In February, 1964, Pavel Zakharov was arrested in Irkutsk. During the search photographs of Nikolai Khmara, who had been tortured to death in prison, and a letter from the Barnaul Church reporting a crime that had been committed, were taken away from him.

The Irkutsk procuracy charged Zakharov with slander on account of the above-mentioned documents, and brought him to trial under article 70 of the Criminal Code of the RSFSR. Zakharov was sentenced to three years in labor camp, strict regime. He was sent to the Potma labor camp in Mordovia. At that time brother N.P. Khrapov was serving a sentence in this camp, and there were also several other Evangelical Christian-Baptist believers there. It was from there that Pavel Zakharov sent us his letter. It was hidden in a shoe and carried out of the camp.

In December, 1964, Pavel Zakharov was released and rehabilitated by a resolution of the Supreme Soviet of the USSR dated November 10, 1964, "In the absence of *corpus delicti.*"

Thus the veracity of the letter from the Barnaul Church and the authenticity of the photographs of brother Khmara who was tortured for his faith were officially and legally corroborated.

At this period the church was urgently praying and energetically petitioning outsiders for the release of Christian prisoners. Delegations of believers from many local Evangelical Christian-Baptist communities arrived in Moscow: from Kiev, Brest, Bryansk, Chelyabinsk, Barnaul, and other towns. As a rule the delegations were not large, about five to ten men.

In 1964 the Council of Prisoners' Relatives of the Evangelical Christian-Baptist Church was formed in defense of those convicted for the Word of God. The Council sent direct petitions to the Procuracy of the USSR. In 1964, throughout almost six months, representatives of the Organizing Committee of Evangelical Christian-Baptists were to be found in the waiting-room of the Central Committee of the Communist Party of the Soviet Union with petitions against the intervention of the Council for the Affairs of Religious Cults and other bodies in the internal church life of the whole Evangelical-Baptist brotherhood.

In the second half of 1964 began the rehabilitation and release of Evangelical Christian-Baptist prisoners. At the beginning of 1965 almost all of them had been released, with the exception of a few people. The Lord had answered His people's prayers. The Church of God rejoiced and praised its Heavenly Father.

"When the Lord restored the fortunes of Zion, we were like those who dream. Then our mouth was filled with laughter, and our tongue with shouts of joy; then they said among the nations, 'The Lord has done great things for them.' The Lord has done great things for us; we are glad" (Ps. 126: 1-3).

Those coming out of prison joined zealously in the labor in God's harvest field. Returning from prison in December, 1964, Pavel Zakharov visited many churches of our brotherhood, calling upon his fellow-believers to act unanimously for the faith of the Gospel.

During this period he did much work through Siberia, and accomplished visits to many churches in the Northern Caucasus. He gave a great deal of his energy and attention to the local church in Prokopievsk.

In 1966, however, a new period of persecution began. In 1966 new decrees directed against believers were published. In the provinces new arrests of believers and open persecution began. In May, 1966, a large delegation of Evangelical Christian-Baptist believers arrived in Moscow. Among them was Pavel Zakharov, as a delegate from the believers of Prokopievsk. At ten o'clock in the morning in front of the main entrance to the building of the Central Committee of the CPSU, there suddenly appeared a large delegation of believers numbering about 500 people. The delegation spent two days and one night outside of the Central Committee Building, petitioning for all those persecuted and oppressed for their faith. On May 17, 1966, the peaceful delegation of believers was arrested and taken to Lefortovo prison in Moscow. Among those arrested was Pavel Zakharov.

On June 23, 1966, the Pervomaisky People's Court sentenced Zakharov under article 142, section 2 of the Criminal Code of the RSFSR, to three years in labor camp, intensive regime.

Zakharov spent the last three years of his imprisonment in the town of Nalchik in the Northern Caucasus. His health took an abrupt turn for the worse. When he returned from prison, he spent many months in the hospital.

In October, 1969, a great tragedy overtook him; his wife, Esfir Yakovlevna, died. Their four children were left motherless.

Although he was ill, Pavel Zakharov continued to perform what service he could for the church in Prokopievsk.

In July, 1970, in a hospital in Prokopievsk, Zakharov wrote the article "The Last Supper." I quote a few excerpts from his article:

242

We wait for His appearance and the rapture of the Church—His Bride. Wait thus for Christ at all times, as long as there is breath in you and you can hear the beating of your heart in your decrepit body.

O dear friend, brother and sister! Awake!

And now while you still hear the voice of the Merciful One, who is patiently awaiting your return, return quickly! Fall down before Him! Bring the talent the Lord has given you with the profit that pleases Him. He expects sacrificial service from you, from me, and from everyone who comes to His house. The Church prays to the Lord for her servants, who so much need His strength and leadership. She prays that the Lord will still raise up worthy servants for His vineyard.

The Church prays to the Lord that the Gospel may spread and be preached everywhere, and rejoices because for her witness to Christ she suffers contempt, imprisonment, exile, and every kind of deprivation from the world. She thanks her heavenly Father for the strength of the Spirit of God, which gives victory over every dishonor and evil.

This was his spiritual testament to the Prokopievsk church and the whole Evangelical Christian-Baptist brotherhood.

In 1971, Pavel Zakharov's state of health worsened abruptly and on July 1, 1971, he passed away.

Pavel Zakharov walked along a difficult but faithful path. Selflessly he sowed the seeds of God's eternal truth among the Russian people. Thousands of people heard his sermons and his calls to faithfulness to the Lord.

In prison cells and labor camps among the prisoners he bore a fearless testimony to God's love. They respected Pavel Zakharov and affectionately named him "Dad."

"May those who sow in tears reap with shouts of joy! He that goes forth weeping, bearing the seed for sowing, shall come home with shouts of joy, bringing his sheaves with him" (Ps. 126: 5, 6).

These verses also relate to Pavel Zakharov. He is now in Heaven with the Lord. The tears and sorrows of the earthly path have remained far behind. The sheaves of his labor are before the Lord. There he waits for us, too, his friends and comrades in evangelistic labor.

He has already found rest from his labors, but for us storms and tempests and toil lie in wait on the path to eternity!

13

Alexandra Mozgova

ON MARCH 9, 1972, IN MOSCOW, Alexandra Ivanovna Mozgova passed into eternity at the age of 67. The Lord called this tireless and faithful laborer to His everlasting dwelling-place.

She turned to the Lord when she was sixteen and began to labor in His vineyard. During the time of the revolution she recited invocatory poems on the squares of Moscow in front of large crowds of listeners. In those years the preaching of Christ overflowed like a broad river across the plains of Russia. Thousands of sinners turned to Christ.

In 1926 Alexandra Ivanovna began to work in the office of the Federal Union of Christians Baptists in Moscow. All the work of the Baptist Union in those years was subordinated to two chief tasks: the evangelization of the country and the inner spiritual education of the swiftly growing Evangelical Christian-Baptist brotherhood.

Alexandra Ivanovna was greatly influenced spiritually by Nikolai Odintsov, Pavel Datsko, Pavel Ivanov-Klyshnikov, and others. Throughout her life she retained not only radiant memories of them, but also faithfulness to the Holy Gospel for which they had given their lives. She often remembered their fervent prayers, their zealous, selfless service, their deep personal attachment to one another.

After 1929, when the blows of persecution fell upon our brotherhood, and the leaders of the Baptist Union were subjected to particularly intense pressure on the part of the authorities, Nikolai Odintsov would often gather his colleagues in the office around him after a regular summons to the secret police, share with them the difficulties which had arisen, and pray fervently with them for the dear brotherhood. He taught his brothers and sisters who worked with him steadfastness and courage in upholding the things of God. When the blows of persecution affected each of Odintsov's colleagues personally, his young sister-colleagues almost all went to prison, but kept their faithfulness to Christ.

My parents knew Alexandra Ivanovna well. In 1930, during the work of the Plenum of the Baptist Union in Moscow, my father and mother stayed in her flat at 9 Rubtsovy Lane. The same year my father was arrested in that flat . . .

A few decades later I also had the opportunity to make Alexandra Ivanovna's acquaintance. With great emotion I crossed the threshold of the old Moscow flat where my father's prison journey had begun in 1930.

Nikolai Odintsov and Alexandra Ivanovna were arrested almost simultaneously in November 1933.

During the investigation she maintained total silence about the life of our brotherhood. She was sentenced together with Odintsov to three years. She served her term in a camp for the construction of the White Sea-Baltic canal in the Medvezhegorsk district. A. Ananin, the Chairman of the Siberian Christian-Baptist Union, also served his sentence there. Alexandra Ivanovna was able to see documents, the "Statutes" and the "Letters of Instruction to Senior Presbyters." In 1960 the All-Union Council carried out a purge of its staff. Alexandra Ivanovna was pensioned off.

In 1961 the work of the Action Group of the Evangelical Christians Baptists was begun. Alexandra Ivanovna followed it attentively and with deep sympathy, praying fervently to the Lord for the revival of the Evangelical-Baptist brotherhood, and then she herself began to help the friends of the revival. During 1965 and 1966 she greatly helped the Council of Evangelical Christian-Baptist Churches with typewriting work, especially at the time when the Regulations of the Council of Churches were being worked out. Alexandra Ivanovna played an active part in the "Herald of Salvation," the journal of the revived brotherhood of Evangelical Christians Baptists. She gleaned a great deal of material for the journal. She carefully preserved a whole series of manuscripts of articles and poetry written by evangelical laborers of past years, and subsequently handed them over to the Council of Churches.

A member of the registered Evangelical Christian-Baptist community in Moscow, Alexandra Ivanovna upheld Evangelical-Baptist principles. Often she exposed the leadership of the All-Union Council and the leaders of the local Moscow community in deviations from the Gospel. But her quiet, faint voice was often raised alone . . .

In 1966, when numerous trials of supporters of the Council of Churches were taking place in Moscow, Alexandra Ivanovna was present at almost every trial, praying for every prisoner.

She knew the history of our brotherhood well, loved the Lord ardently, and saw in the Council of Churches movement the continuation of that great work of the Gospel to which Prokhanov, Odintsov, Ivanov-Klyshnikov, Datsko and many others had entirely dedicated themselves.

Alexandra Ivanovna lived a long, fruitful life, totally dedicated to the Lord.

In conclusion I shall quote excerpts from Alexandra Ivanovna's album. For many decades she kept an album with entries and good wishes from many believers. It opens on March 11, 1929, with an entry from a student on a Bible course—Brother Borets.

The spring of 1929 was the threshold of persecution. The Lord was preparing His Church for its trials. These precious brotherly entries and good wishes, preserved since the 1930's, reveal to us now the exalted spirit of the champions of the Gospel, their courage, and the depth of their faith. Their courageous summons to faithfulness is especially dear to us, the believers of today.

FROM ALEXANDRA MOZGOVA'S ALBUM

March 11, 1929
"Follow me" (John 21: 22).
The Lord is now opening before His children the

fiery door of trial. We can already hear the echoes of the many-visaged beast: "To the stake with them!" The children of God must learn in reality what it means "to be hated by all men." But let not our hearts be troubled, for as He opens this door to us He Himself goes with us, and therefore, as the first Christians did, we too can say: "You can kill us, but you cannot harm us!"

And so let us rejoice, my dear friend Alexandra Ivanovna, that the Lord accords us the honor of participation in the afflictions of His body, so that we may subsequently be participants in His marvelous glory."

> N. Borets
> Moscow,
> Baptist Bible Course

March 9, 1929
"A truthful witness saves lives" (Prov. 14: 25).

> V.I. Sinitsin
> Moscow

March 10, 1929
Dear sister Shura!

With our present experiences and feelings, I somehow cannot find it in my heart to write anything joyful. But when I write in someone's album I want only to express sincere and heartfelt good wishes for their journey along our hard Christian path.

My dear sister, you have already begun to walk along this difficult, sorrow-filled path. Understand then that if you are faithful to the end to your Lord, then also to the end you will not meet with compassion from this world, nor will you find that it understands you. Do not forget this one thing, that in order for God to love us, the world must hate us; in order to be accepted by Heaven we will without fail be exiles here. There is no place for us here, there is no cool shade, no shelter to rest from our labors, and this is all so that we shall be received by Heaven and have a place there.

But this is the world, and when you start to draw near to Golgotha, then even your friends can desert you. One can often encounter this on the Christian path. When all this overtakes you on the path, do not cease to be faithful to the Lord and to serve Him. Bear offenses patiently as though they were not heavy. Forgive everyone. If your friends desert you and your heart is heavy, then weep quietly alone with the Lord, and it will be lighter. Be affectionate and gentle to everyone, and may your meekness and humility, which all of us should possess at all times, be known to everyone. Love everyone with brotherly love, and each person will see Christ in your soul and in your eyes. Always be bold before everyone you meet in this ministry, because in this high calling is our mission.

Labor with success and be happy.

V.G. Lobkov
(FROM SIBERIA)

March 9, 1929
Dear sister in the Lord Mozgova:
"To him who conquers I will grant to eat of the

tree of life, which is in the paradise of God . . . "
(Rev. 2: 7).

F. Sapozhnikov
Moscow

March 11, 1929

The Lord said: "I will never fail you nor forsake you" (Heb. 13: 5), and "I will not leave you desolate" (John 14: 18).

The Lord is faithful to His promises.

Your brother in the Lord,
I. Ya. Miller

August 3, 1930

"These are they who were not defiled . . . who follow after the Lamb, . . . they are redeemed from among men . . . they sing as it were a new song . . . the song of the redeemed from the earth."

I sincerely wish that you may learn this song and strive with all your heart toward that place, so that you may join those standing before the throne and singing a new song.

He "by the power at work within us is able to do far more abundantly than all that we ask or think" (Eph. 3: 20).

Dare—believe!

From your brother
in Christ and co-laborer
in His harvest field,
G. Shalye
Moscow

251

December 13, 1932

Three wonderful promises:
"It is the Lord who goes before you,
He will be with you,
He will not fail you."

(Deut. 31: 8)

The first is a sure pledge of security.

The second is an inexhaustible fount of encouragement and consolation.

The third is a reliable guarantee of unfailing love.

He will go before you everywhere, will be with you always, will never fail you.

N. Odintsov

January 4, 1936

A good memory of our meeting in exile

People enter in an album such words as will serve as an expression of the best wishes in life for a person who is close to them in the aspirations whose principles draw them together. These wishes reflect the sentiments and experiences of the present writer.

When I hear wonderful stories about the life and work of individuals who have set themselves as their highest aim the fulfillment of the will of Him who sent us into this life, I am enraptured by their ardent and inspired transports of spirit, pressing them on to superhuman feats of self-sacrifice in the name of the Lord Jesus Christ, the Savior of the world, and for the sake of the good and the salvation of their neighbors.

Firm faith in God and devotion to Him to the end (Rev. 2: 10); unshakable courage in actions and in various experiences, courage which accompanied all the heroic martyrs of radiant Christianity down the centuries as they marched joyfully to Golgotha; perfect Christian love, the foundation and abundant source of virtue in its different manifestations; bright hope in the previous promises of our Heavenly Father (John 14: 23) which instills quiet rest, joy and peace into the heart; this was the substance of the lives of all those who followed the Leader and Savior of the world—the Lord Jesus Christ.

And to you, dear sister in the Lord, Alexandra Ivanovna, with a sincere heart I wish that you may acquire from the Almighty Lord God those lofty Christian values which serve as an adornment of the life of a believing person who is marching to the eternal Canaan.

I.E. Kutumov
KARELIA-SOSNOVSK

APPENDIXES

Appendix I

Georgi Vins' Poetry

Georgi Vins' poetry is primarily of personal and confessional rather than literary value. We have therefore thought it better to give a prose translation than to attempt verse translations. The following brief notes outline the formal properties of the poems. We also attach short extracts from the poems in English transliteration, so that those who are able may form their own judgments of Vins' poetry.

"My Labor Camp Diary." All the poems in this chapter are regularly rhymed, with alternating feminine and masculine rhymes; mostly aBaB, but in a few cases AbAb, and in one case aaBccB. (Capital letters—masculine rhymes.)

Like most 20th century Russian poets, Vins uses some slant-rhymes or off-rhymes (nepolniye rifmy); e.g., narodu/svobody; kronu/poklonom;

slovo/surovykh; mirom/kumiru; nauchen/tuchi;
bezdelya/tselyu; dorozhe/mnozhit.

His meters are classical, mainly iambic pen-
tameter, with some iambic hexameters, and at least
one iambic tetrameter. Some of the meters are
anapaestic, others dactylic, at least one trochaic.

THE MESSIAH
(stanzas 3, 7 and 8.)

3. On izvedal stradanya i slezy
   I byl raspyat zlobnoi tolpoi.
   Ne ob etom li plachut beryozy
   Sokom svetlym rannei vesnoi?

7. Yest strana na zemlye—Rossiya,
   Yest v nei vernye Bogu syny,
   Nezametniye lyudi, prostiye,
   No Khristovoi siloi polny!

8. Vera v Boga rekoyu moguchei
   Po prostoram Rossii techet,
   Drug lyudei—Iisus—samy luchshii
   Prizyvaet k spasenyu narod!

MY LOVE AND MY SONG IS RUSSIA
(stanzas 3, 4 and 5.)

3. Pridet pora: vesenniye luchi
   Rastopyat sneg i les raseravit kronu
   I pobegut taezhniye ruchi
   K bolshoi vode s privetom i poklonom.

4. Zazeleneyut rechek berega
   I veter zaigraet nad volnami . . .
   I detvoroi odenutsya luga,
   Kak yarkimi i sochnymi tsvetami.

5. I staya zhuravlei, spuskayasya k ruchyu,
   Krichit, privetstvuya kraya rodniye . . .
   V vesennii den vostorzhenno shepchu:
   Moya lyubov i pesn moya—Rossiya!

Appendix II

Letters

(This letter shows the sufferings of the third generation of the Vins family, who are already following in the steps of their parents and grandparents.)

To: A.N. Kosygin, the Kremlin, Moscow
    N. V. Podgorny, the Kremlin, Moscow
Copies to: Council of Churches of Evangelical
                Christians and Baptists
                Council of ECB Prisoners' Relatives

April 18, 1974

In violation of the Constitution of the USSR and of international conventions on human rights, our father, Georgi Petrovich Vins, has again been illegally arrested for his religious convictions and his work in the Church.

For thirteen years our father has constantly been subject to persecutions from the authorities. He served a term of imprisonment from 1966 to 1969, from which he returned with his health seriously undermined. This new arrest causes us to fear for his life. We do not want to see our Father posthumously rehabilitated like our grandfather, Pyotr Yakovlevich Vins, who was sentenced for his religious convictions and tortured to death in the camps, but later rehabilitated.

Our whole family has been suffering persecutions for many years now. Our grandmother, Lidia Mikhailovna Vins, served a term in the camps from 1970 to 1973 because she campaigned for our father during his imprisonment and for other believers who had suffered repressions. Our mother, Mrs. N.I. Vins, was dismissed from her job in 1962 because of her religious convictions, and for some years she was unable to get work anywhere. She is now working, but not in her own profession.

The repressions also affect us children. Natasha Vins was illegally dismissed from work on January 9, 1974. During a preliminary conversation the senior doctor of Kiev Hospital No. 17, Khryapa, declared that he would find a pretext for dismissing her, since religion and medicine were incompatible. Petya Vins has finished the tenth form [i.e., he is now 17—Ed.] but cannot find work anywhere.

All actions against our family are an attempt to annihilate us. Our father's present arrest is impermissible, and if you do not release him immediately, we will take all possible steps, beginning with an appeal to all believers, telling them what has happened.

We have full reason to suppose that he is in bad

health. All responsibility for his life and continued imprisonment rests with you. If our father is not released and if measures are taken against him in prison which endanger his health, then we want to inform you and believers throughout the world that our whole family is fully resolved to die with him.

> Natasha Vins
> Petya (Peter) Vins
> Liza Vins
> Zhenya (Eugene) Vins
> KIEV-114,
> UL. SOSHENKE 11B.

September 11, 1974
To the World Council of Churches, Amsterdam

I ask you to intercede for Georgi Petrovich Vins, the well-known religious figure, the Baptist, who was elected by his fellow believers as Secretary of the Council of Evangelical Christian and Baptist Churches.

Vins, like other members of his family, has several times been arrested and subjected to other illegal persecutions. Recently he has been compelled to hide from the threat of another arrest. In March 1974, Vins was arrested in Kiev and charged with vagrancy. Protesting against this arbitrariness, he has already, for more than four months, been on a hunger strike, which is threatening his life. The trial is expected in the coming weeks, and he is once again threatened with a prison sentence.

Vins enjoys enormous authority and love among

his fellow believers. By interceding in his defense you will be helping all the Evangelical Christians and Baptists who have been persecuted for many years by the authorities in the worst traditions of religious intolerance of the Middle Ages and of the Tsarist authorities in the time of Pobedonostsev, in the 1890's.

The arrests, breakings-up of prayer meetings, fines, discriminations in schools and at work, and, as the height of inhumanity, the taking away of children from their parents—all this is the lot of the Baptists, and to one degree or another of many religious groups who are inconvenient to the authorities (Uniates, Pentecostals, members of the "True Orthodox Church" and several other groups).

These illegalities demand the intervention of the worldwide public.

Freedom of conscience is an individual part of freedom as a whole. Honest people throughout the world should defend the victims of retigious persecutions wherever these take place—in tiny Albania or in the vast Soviet Union.

Andrei Sakharov,
Academician
Moscow

September 29, 1974
To the International League for the Rights of Man
From Lidia Mikhailovna Vins,
Ul. Soshenka 11b,
Kiev, USSR

I ask you to take whatever measures you can to

free my son Georgi Petrovich Vins (born 1928), who has been in prison in Kiev for 6 months for his religious beliefs.

The prosecutor's office which has been handling the investigation told us that he is to be charged under articles 138/II, 187/I, and 209/I of the Ukrainian Penal Code (corresponding to articles 142/II, 190/I, and 227/I in the Russian) and that there may be a charge also under article 214 of the Ukrainian Penal Code (209 in the Russian).

My son was elected by *Evangelical Christian and Baptist* believers to the Council of Churches of ECBs. In accordance with the laws of our country, the authorities were informed about this; nevertheless he was subjected to persecutions and in 1966 he was arrested and sentenced to three years.

After his release in May 1969, my son continued to serve in the Council of Churches. According to the law, ministers of the church are not obliged to take up secular work. However, as soon as my son was released, the authorities began to demand that he get a job, *notwithstanding* even the fact that three years of imprisonment has so damaged his health that after his release he had to undergo two operations. He still hadn't fully recovered from his time in the camp and from the two operations when they demanded that he get a job; in December 1969, he was suddenly sentenced to a year's forced labor [i.e., obliged to work at a certain place while living at home].

As a minister of the Council of Churches and of the local church, my son sometimes had to make journeys to other churches; he began to do this in his free time. The authorities forbade the journeys; they forbade him to attend prayer meetings; and several times the police detained him at prayer meetings in his own church.

In December 1969, he was called to the prosecutor's office. In the summons it stated that there was a fresh charge against him under article 209 of the Ukrainian Penal Code (227 in the Russian)—as it turned out later, for a sermon he gave at the wedding of two members of our church. It was stated that the sermon contained appeals for antisocial activity. We have a tape rcording of that sermon and we can make it available to you if necessary.

After receiving the summons from the prosecutor's office, my son informed the authorities that he could not carry on his Christian ministry under such conditions and that he was transferring to full-time Christian ministry. An all-Union search was launched for him.

In March 1974, my son was arrested in the Urals and is now in prison in Kiev.

Article 227 of the Russian Penal Code (209 in the Ukrainian) says: "The organization or leadership of a group, whose activity is carried on under the guise of the preaching of religious doctrines and the fulfillment of religious rituals, and is connected with the causing of harm to citizens' health or with other violations of citizens' personality or rights, or with motivating citizens to refuse social activity or the fulfillment of civil obligations, and also with the enticement of minors into this group—is punishable by imprisonment for a period of up to five years, or exile for the same period, or by corrective labor for a period of up to one year."

According to article 227 of the Russian Penal

Code, the period of imprisonment is up to five years, or alternatively exile, but according to article 209 of the Ukrainian Penal Code and in some other republics they can give up to five years' imprisonment plus five years' exile.

This article began to be widely applied to believers of our denomination from 1961. Sentences under this article were not only completely unfounded in law, but they were absurd, and from 1964 they virtually stopped applying it. This was a time when the persecutions were slackening, but in March 1966 the decree was adopted about the reinforcement of article 138 of the Ukrainian Penal Code (142 in the Russian) and article 187/I of the Ukrainian Penal Code (190/I in the Russian) was adopted. After this, believers began to be sentenced under these articles, chiefly under article 138 (142). The believers were not guilty of violating these articles either and they wrote to the authorities about this frequently. Now they have begun to apply article 209 of the Ukrinian Penal Code because under articles 138 and 187/I they can only sentence a man to three years' imprisonment, but under article 209 they can give five years' imprisonment and five years' exile. Thus, under this article they can deprive a man of freedom for ten years. This is the only reason why they have begun to apply article 209 of the Ukrainian Penal Code (and corresponding articles in other republics).

My son is charged under three articles of the Ukrainian Penal Code: 209/I, 138/II, and 187/I.

He is charged as a minister of the Council of Churches. As we were told in the prosecutor's office the charge is based on the "Fraternal Leaflets" [the bimonthly bulletin of the Council of Churches], letters and appeals of the Council of Churches to the believers.

These "Fraternal Leaflets" and letters of the Council of Churches contain nothing illegal. You can assure yourselves of this if you look at all the materials involved in the case.

I beg you to investigate this matter and help in the release of my son.

Please do something immediately, because the investigation on the case has ended and they may even conceal the day of the trial from us.

Yours sincerely,
Lidia Mikhailovna Vins,
mother

September 29, 1974
To the "Amnesty International" organization
From Lidia Mikhailovna Vins, ul. Soshenka 11b,
Kiev 114, USSR.

A few days ago I sent you a letter asking you to petition for the release of my son Georgi Petrovich Vins, born in 1928, who has been in prison in Kiev for 6 months for his religious beliefs.

He is to be charged under articles 138/II, 187/I of the Ukrainian Penal Code, 209/I of the Ukrainian Penal Code (142/II, 190/I and 227/I of the Russian) and the procuracy investigator said that he may also be charged under article 214 of the Ukrainian Penal Code (209 of the Russian).

The investigation in this case has now been finished and the trial could take place in the very near future. Therefore I appeal to you again and ask you to send your representative immediately, since the trial may begin very soon indeed without our being informed in advance.

I also ask that your representative should have a meeting with my son G. P. Vins, and request that all the materials of the case against my son be made available to your committee.

Yours sincerely,
Lidia Mikhailovna Vins,
mother

October 22, 1974
To the World Council of Churches,
to Amnesty International.

At his forthcoming trial in Kiev, Georgi Petrovich Vins, the General Secretary of the Council of Evangelical Christians-Baptists (sic), will be charged under article 209/I of the Criminal Code of the Ukrainian SSR: "Infringement of the person and rights of citizens under the pretext of fulfilling religious rites or under other pretext."

This article has recently begun to be used against Baptists. Apparently the authorities are attracted by the long term of punishment which is allowed under it: five years' imprisonment plus five years' exile—more than under other articles previously used against Baptists.

What citizens' rights has Mr. Vins infringed, and whose rights? Certainly not the rights of those several thousand Baptists of the Soviet Union who signed an appeal to the authorities demanding Mr. Vins' release. Apparently the charge will be constructed on the basis of the fact that Mr. Vins was not working in the service of the state. From this will be indirectly drawn the conclusion that he was living on the means of believers and, in this way, infringing their material rights.

However, in the first place, it is obvious and well known that the church puts no compulsion on the believers to contribute money. And in the second place, how can the authorities make such charges when, for their devotion to God, believers are fined thousands of rubles, all their religious literature (in fact any text which contains the word "God") is confiscated during hundreds of house searches and destroyed, the music and texts of the Psalms are confiscated, musical instruments are destroyed, prayer houses are razed, parents have their children removed from them, and any education beyond secondary school is barred to young believers?

The authorities cannot be reconciled with the fact of the existence of the Christian Church, whose servants do not follow the directions of the bureaucrats of the Committee for the Affairs of Religious Cults. The fact of the authorities' struggle with the free church, including the help of article 209/I of the Criminal Code of the Ukrainian SSR (there have already been more than ten trials in 1974), shows that the authorities are grossly infringing the generally accepted rights of believers while cynically pretending to protect their rights.

A. Sakharov
G. Podyapolsky
S. Kovalyov
T. Velikanova

Appendix III

**A Personal Report from Lidia M. Vins
About the Trial of Her Son Georgi P. Vins**
February 24, 1975

Before I say anything about the trial, I want to say
that we are very small people. We have done what we
had to do from our youth until today. And the Lord
has done great things: in the midst of great dangers
and persecutions, He has caused it to happen that
"we were considered as dead and behold we live." By
His mercy we have remained alive. And if we should
speak about all the sufferings, then it is the story of
all our people, of our Christians. As one of our songs
says: "Whoever has come through struggles and
tears." We are very small people, but the Lord has
done great things not only through our sufferings,
but through the sufferings of all His children who
have been particularly faithful to Him for many
years and especially in the last decades.

The hardest thing among all these sufferings, especially when you are in camp or in prison, is to realize that you are alone. That everybody in the whole world has forgotten you. And then the Lord is with you as the most faithful friend and the realization that God's children were praying always revived us, brought us back to life and gave us new strength. Many who have been in prison have testified that they felt people's prayers and they knew not simply those days when they were prayed for, but the actual hours. This is the testimony of more than one prisoner. It was the same with me, too. And it was the same with my son who said at the trial: "I felt the prayers of God's children and these prayers gave me strength and brought me back to life." We are wholeheartedly grateful first to the Lord for His faithfulness and also to the Christians of the whole world for their prayers. At those times when it was very difficult, in those moments when it seemed that everything was finished, just one thought or one word that someone was praying for us was able to encourage us and bring us back to life, and we were able to continue on our path.

I am very moved by the many prayers that have been made for us and I am not surprised that my son, when he went, so to speak, through the fire, when he was under attack, still felt very calm, very courageous, very decisive. When I saw him during the trial, tormented and pale, with sunken eyes, I thought: he hasn't slept for nights. The trial lasted five days. But when we parted he said: "I was able to go to sleep peacefully every night. It was a very great mercy of God. It is surely due to the many prayers of God's children." It was the same with me too. When there had been a prayer day, especially after a Sunday, and everyone expected that I would be unable to get up because of my state of health, to everyone's amazement I did get up and walk, and I knew it was only because of the prayers of God's children. And it was only through those prayers that God gave me life and health and strength, so that I was able to leave imprisonment unharmed, to the amazement of all the atheists.

Of ourselves we do not deserve these things. But we are so happy that we can represent our whole suffering brotherhood. If people pray for us, care for us, speak up for us, then they have done it for all. They have done it for those who are resolved to remain true to the Lord until death, and there are more than a few thousand such.

Now I want to describe the court situation in a few words. The trial was kept secret from us. When we learned about it, and on that account wrote to the government that through Voss we had got A. Haerem as our defending lawyer, they called me in specially and spoke to me very politely (although normally they are always very rough) saying that we should accept an atheist to make our defense. We refused. We said it would not be very nice to invite someone else before telling the one who had already been asked. And that is what happened. This lawyer, Alf Haerem, remained our defense lawyer throughout. And every time my son was supposed to answer a question he would say: "I'll answer that question when my defense lawyer Alf Haerem is here, or he'll answer himself.'"

Well, to tell everything that happened at the trial would take a long time. Also it would be very difficult and painful. Briefly I can say that it was not a court tribunal—it was an act of violence. And it is difficult for me to describe the external circumstances or even the contents of the trial, for they kept it secret from us. But the Lord enabled us to learn of the day of the trial. The building was surrounded by strong army forces and it was simply impossible to get through. This was true not only for the believers or anyone else, but even for his family. During the trial we managed with great difficulty to get into the courtroom. Very many hindrances had been set up. But we have no time to describe all the minutiae of this. Everybody was pushed away from the building to the other side of the street, and Christians and those who wanted to attend the trial stood out there for days on end, in frost and cold, waiting till the trial ended.

So the trial began, and he was asked whether he nad any refusals to the court. The first question affected the lawyer, an atheist state official. My son rejected him and said he had agreed he could not defend him. Then we were invited to say what the situation was regarding the advocate from Norway. I handed in a statement. The advocate was willing to come, but he had not been given an entry visa. Then my son rejected the whole court presidium on the grounds that: 1. It is a one-sided atheist court. It is not I who am on trial, but the whole ECB Christian faith. The Bible, the Gospel, our whole movement is on trial. 2. The investigation had taken place with extreme violence, with the use of physical and mental terror. The investigation had not been conducted by state lawyers but by the KGB. One of their workers had threatened him over a period of two months, and there he is in the fourth row, on the fourth chair at the end, and his name is . . . He went on to say that a man had been put in his cell who over a period of two and a half months threatened to strangle and kill him. Thus he was unable to participate in the investigation. The court rejected this accusation.

He then stated that he would not participate in the trial and asked that his requests be accepted. These consisted of 18 points. The first point requested the court to admit an advocate, e. g., Alf Haerem, as a believer. The second request was that a scientific and Christian investigation be prepared with the participation of a Christian lawyer. Since we do not have any such in this country, it must be representatives from other countries. For in the atheist experts' findings, several chapters of the Bible were described as anti-state and even criminal. In this way the court has confirmed that it is not directed against me. My friends and relatives should understand that I do not ask for a lawyer on my own account, but in order to justify and defend our whole brotherhood and our faith, what it is based and built on, since the whole world accepts it, just as the Bible is accepted worldwide.

His requests also included the formation of a special commission to be composed of members of the leadership of the KGB, of the department for religious affairs, and representatives of the Council of Prisoners' Relatives, to investigate whether accusations put forward in his name from the whole brotherhood were false. Also that the tribunal investigating his case should request from Moscow a review of the number of Christians imprisoned between 1929 and 1945 and how many of these died in imprisonment. The same for the period 1945 to 1974. Also how much Christian literature was confiscated, including Bibles, New Testaments, and hymnbooks. How many Christians were excluded from higher education on various pretexts. How many prayer houses were destroyed between 1929 and 1974. How many Christian parents were deprived of their parental rights, and other questions relating to the position of Christians.

The president of the court was partial in his cross-examination of the witnesses. None of the witnesses requested by my son were permitted into the court. During cross-examination of the witnesses, particular questions were asked, geared toward the intended sentence. After this type of cross-examination, he was asked to state his opinion. He said he would only make a statement in the case of a thorough investigation in the presence of his defense lawyer Alf Haerem. He would make no statements in these conditions. But he did give an explanation, saying: "I insist that here in our country a campaign of annihilation is being waged against Christians. Since you have refused to obtain the facts, I can tell you that from 1929 to 1945, 25,000 Christians were imprisoned and 22,000 died in the camps. From 1945 to 1974, 20,000 were imprisoned and 6,000 were excluded from higher education. Since 1929, 10 million books have been confiscated. These are the main points, indicating that even today Christians are being physically annihilated in the camps and prisons.

"I could be at home today. From the first day of my imprisonment onward I was invited to collaborate with the security police within the Council of

Churches; then I could go home to my children. But I refused. Now I know that the Lord permitted it, and I accept from His hand anything He wants."

Then the experts spoke. In fact the whole of the experts' findings was not read out. My son was accused of:

Falsifying Soviet reality. There was no persecution here. His story "Faithfulness" had been published in various news releases of the Council of Prisoners' Relatives and in other places. This history of Christianity was directed against the state; it was criminal and contained lies. In this story he described the life of several leaders of the Christians (Baptists) in recent times, their sermons and letters. Then there was the "Family Chronicle" about the fate of his father, his mother, his uncle, etc. In the experts' findings, they had accused him of acting against the state and appealing for rejection of the legal order, but they had not found this proven. The president of the court suggested since they had heard the testimony of the witnesses, could they not improve this and write that such appeals had been recorded on tape? They agreed.

Then my son was given an opportunity for defense. He said: "My defense should be conducted by Alf Haerem. But now I leave my whole case with my Lord Jesus Christ." Then the state counsel spoke. A sentence of five years' camp and five years' exile in Siberia, with confiscation of property, was proposed. Then he was given a last word. But since he did not take part in the trial and his requests had been rejected, he replied: "The last word belongs to my Lord Jesus Christ, who said: I am the Alpha and the Omega, the beginning and the end." That was all.

The sentence was announced the next day. When it was read out to him and they asked: "Have you understood?" He said: "Yes. Glory to Jesus Christ."

Then Christians gave his relatives flowers—roses, carnations, narcissi. Until then the flowers had been concealed under their clothes. These flowers were thrown to him His son took them and threw them, saying: "Daddy, these are for you and your bravery." His wife threw flowers to him, saying: "You have won this trial." Also his daughter. The whole room clapped. When the flowers were thrown, everyone fell silent. The whole room was full of people with invitation cards. They applauded and laughed. His daughter Natasha climbed on a seat and said: "No, Daddy, the church will not die [a reference to one of his poems], just as the love of Christ does not die. With Christ you are free in prison. And freedom without Him is prison."

Usually he was led out last, but this time first. He went out carrying the flowers and saying: "Greetings to all friends." By this time there were more than 500 believers outside the building and about 200 who had come by bus and tram. They were all waiting for this moment and holding bouquets of flowers. But he was secretly led out another way. Then all the believers removed their headgear and began to sing. It was very moving. The group of 500 sang—everybody sang. Everything was still; no one moved. Then I came out with my grandson, leaning on his arm. He took off his cap, as at a funeral. They opened up to let us through and we made our way back home. But the day before all the young people had gone through the back entrance to the place where his prison car stood. And he heard them singing the song: "For the faith of the Gospel . . ." Police came up, but nothing could be done until he was taken away. This was the trial.

Four days later a reunion was permitted. His wife and son met him, only two persons were permitted and the three small children. They did not allow me or his daughter to go in. The reunion took place through a glass door or wall, and there were telephone booths through which they spoke to him. The conversation was certainly overheard; they couldn't discuss anything special. He said: "I didn't want to hand in the appeal." But we asked him to do it. Not to get him off, but to demonstrate that a higher instance would pass the same sentence. We don't know whether he handed it in or not; this is being concealed from us. Today [Monday] a parcel was taken to him. I don't know whether he's there or not. But at the reunion he asked for warm clothing. They probably told him that he would be in deepest Siberia. He asked for very warm clothing.

But what will the Lord do now? We are full of anticipation. I recall that the whole world, all Christians, are concerned for us. We do not deserve it. And this flag of victory belongs first to the Lord and then to the quiet, unnoticed martyrs who go silently, many times leaving their large families behind, who prefer to suffer and die rather than deny the Lord. We should talk about these too. Now I ask you to tell all Christians that the greatest thing they can do is pray. If anyone can make an appeal for him, as the Lord permits, we are prepared to accept anything.

And the suffering of our whole brotherhood is expressed through my son's name and all our family. People should not speak about us only, but about all the Christians here, so that they can live freely, if that is the will of our Heavenly Father. And tell this particularly to those who were directly involved in the case, who made a great effort, both brother Voss and others who wanted to take part, who were ready to attend the trial. This is wonderful. We never thought that our desire to have a lawyer from outside would mean so much for Christians of the world and would reveal the truth.

I forgot one important thing. Concerning the matter of a defending lawyer, we were given a meeting at the end of October, where he asked for a Christian defense. That took them by surprise. I was meeting him again after four years of separation . . . When I was released, I was followed by unknown people for five months. They watched every step. I had no chance to go anywhere, because they were after me. They watched my flat. When he was arrested, this surveillance was lifted. That's why I wasn't able to see him for four years.

I met him again in the prison regarding the matter of a defense lawyer. When it was time to leave, we prayed. We had been told beforehand that we must not speak about any matter but that of a defense lawyer. That was in order that he could not speak about how they had treated him and what his situation was now. But when I left, he said: "Mama, bless me." That was all. So we prayed. I blessed him and prayed over him. We did no wrong. But at the trial he said: "After the reunion with my mother I ate and drank nothing for 12 days." He wanted to say what they did with him, but they wouldn't let him. They ordered him to sit down and I don't know what happened. But at the trial he said that he was only able to get up two months out of ten. That's all. For clarity, I would like to repeat the accusations against my son:

1. Violation of the law on religious cults which involves: Ban on all missionary activity, inviting young people into the church, Christian education of children. These are the main points of this article. It is regarded as a criminal article in the USSR.
2. Falsification of Soviet reality through news and information about the persecution and imprisonments of believers.
3. Violations of rights of citizens, e. g., any sermon calling for conversion or, more precisely, any missionary activity. This is the strongest article, which also refers to damaging citizens' health. "Under the pretext of religion, violence is practiced on a person's body and the moral life is destroyed." In contrast to the other two, which entail three years' imprisonment, violation of this article entails ten years: five years' labor camp and five years' exile (Siberia).

For a second sentence, as was the case with my son, prisoners receive an increased punishment: the first parcel (food) is permitted *only after two and a half years;* during these two and a half years he may not receive *any* parcel. *Meetings:* once a year. *Correspondence:* one or two letters a month. These explanations must be added in order to understand why my son and also other believers were sentenced under a convenient pretext. This article has become a welcome basis for sentence because it gives the longest term of imprisonment.

Appendix IV

Vins' Appeal Rejected
May 8, 1975

Further details concerning the case of Georgi Vins, the reform Baptist leader, have been received at Keston College (Centre for the Study of Religion and Communism). The information is taken from a letter of March 26, 1975, which Lidia Vins, Georgi's mother, addressed to the Human Rights Committee and Amnesty International.

On March 5 the Vins family delivered a letter to the Supreme Court of the Ukraine in which they drew attention to the illegality of his trial. Vins had himself already appealed to the Supreme Court against his sentence. The court heard his case on March 6 and rejected the appeal. The family was not informed that the hearing had taken place, nor were they told of the decision until March 19—despite almost daily inquiries. The fact that Vins was in a hospital during this time was also "painstakingly hidden" from them.

The family has also been refused a copy of the official verdict by the Kiev City Court. The judge, a man named Tyshel, claimed that they only wanted a copy in order to send it to the CIA. He described the family as "enemies of the people" and "hoodlums." Now they are being shadowed and the house watched.

Lidia Vins appeals for help in opening a reexamination of the case with the participation of a Christian lawyer and representatives from the Supreme Court of the USSR and Amnesty International.

According to an official note of March 25 sent to Lidia Vins, her son is to serve the rest of his sentence in the Yakutsk Autonomous Republic (Eastern Siberia). His health is reported to be "satisfactory."

Appendix V

Keston College. Society for the Study of Religion and Communism.

Keston College is a research and information center that aims to discover the objective truth about religious life in Eastern Europe and other Communist countries, and to make it widely available to churches, academics, international organizations, and other interested bodies. Our slogan is "The Right to Believe." We work on behalf of those whose right to express their faith is stifled in their own countries.

Keston College publishes a quarterly journal, *Religion in Communistic Lands;* a twice-monthly Keston News Service; a quarterly newsletter, *The Right to Believe;* and many books. It also provides a news service by telex.

Keston College helps believers in the West to pray, to be informed about, and to express their concern for persecuted believers in Eastern Europe. For more information write to:

> Keston College
> Heathfield Road
> Keston
> Kent, BR 2 6BA
> England